Basic Skills for the TOEFL® iBT

Edaan Getzel
Tanya Yaunish

Compass Publishing

Speaking 2

Basic Skills for the TOEFL® iBT 2
Speaking

Edaan Getzel · Tanya Yaunish

© 2008 Compass Publishing

Project Editor: Liana Robinson
Acquisitions Editor: Emily Page
Content Editor: Erik Custer
Copy Editor: Alice Wrigglesworth
Contributing Writers: Iain Binns, Micah Sedillos
Consultants: Lucy Han, Chanhee Park
Cover/Interior Design: Dammora Inc

email: info@compasspub.com
http://www.compasspub.com

ISBN: 978-1-59966-156-8

10 9 8 7 6 5 4 3 2 1
10 09 08

Contents

Introduction to the TOEFL® iBT

What is the TOEFL® test?

The TOEFL® iBT (Test of English as a Foreign Language Internet-based Test) is designed to assess English proficiency in non-native speakers who want to achieve academic success as well as effective communication. It is not meant to test academic knowledge or computer ability; therefore, questions are always based on material found in the test.

The TOEFL® iBT test is divided into four sections:
- Reading
- Speaking
- Listening
- Writing

TOEFL® Scores

TOEFL® scores can be used for:
- Admission into university or college where instruction is in English
- Employers or government agencies who need to determine a person's English ability
- English-learning institutes that need to place students in the appropriate level of English instruction

It is estimated that about 4,400 universities and other institutions require a certain TOEFL® test score for admission.

The exact calculation of a TOEFL® test score is complicated and not necessary for the student to understand. However, it is helpful to know that:
- Each section in the Internet-based test is worth 30 points
- The highest possible score on the iBT is 120 points
- Each institution will have its own specific score requirements

✻ It is very important to check with each institution individually to find out what its admission requirements are.

Registering for the TOEFL® iBT

Students who wish to take the TOEFL® test must get registration information. Registration information can be obtained online at the ETS website. The Internet address is www.ets.org/toefl.

The website provides information such as:
- testing locations
- identification requirements
- registration information
- costs
- other test preparation material
- test center locations

This information will vary depending on the country in which you take the test. Be sure to follow the requirements carefully. If you do not have the proper requirements in order, you may not be able to take the test. Remember that if you register online, you will need to have your credit card information ready.

Introduction to the Speaking Section of the TOEFL® iBT

The purpose of the speaking section is to evaluate your ability to speak coherently on your opinions and experiences as well as on information that you have read or heard.

The speaking questions fall into two categories: independent and integrated.

The prompts for speaking questions on the TOEFL® iBT can be categorized into three types:

Question	Time			
	Reading	Listening	Preparation	Speaking
Independent Q1	---	---	15 seconds	45 seconds
Independent Q2				
Integrated Q3	45 seconds	1-2 minutes	30 seconds	60 seconds
Integrated Q4				
Integrated Q5	---	1-2 minutes	30 seconds	60 seconds
Integrated Q6				

For the two independent speaking questions, you should draw upon your own experiences and knowledge.

For the remaining four speaking questions, you will speak about what you read and/or hear. Your ideas need to be well-organized, and the language you use needs to be accurate enough to be easily understood.

In particular, each question type will require test-takers to organize their ideas and speak toward different goals:

Question	Type	Materials	Description
1	Independent	None	Describe your experience
2	Independent	None	Give your opinion and explain why you think this
3	Integrated	Reading	Restate the opinion of the speaker and the examples used
		Conversation	
4	Integrated	Reading	Explain how the example from the lecture supports/refutes the reading
		Lecture	
5	Integrated	Conversation	Restate suggestions and tell which you think is better
6	Integrated	Lecture	Summarize what you heard

How Speaking Will Be Scored

ETS graders will score test-takers' responses according to the following scale:

Score	General Description	Key Points
4	The response answers the question or prompt well. The speaker is easy to understand and there are only minor mistakes with grammar or pronunciation.	Fluent speech that is easy to understand and follow, appropriate use of grammar and vocabulary, ideas explained clearly
3	The response answers the question or prompt, but not all of the ideas are fully developed. The speaker can be understood, but there are some noticeable mistakes in speaking.	At least two (2) of these problems: pronunciation, pace of speech, wrong word choice, limited use of grammar structures, or incorrect grammar
2	The response gives only a basic or minimal answer to the prompt. Most sentences can be understood, but some effort is required by the listener because speech is not fluent and pronunciation is not accurate. Some ideas are not clearly explained.	At least two (2) of these problems: the speech is choppy (not fluent), there are mistakes in pronunciation, word choice is incorrect, only basic grammar is used, grammar is used poorly, only basic ideas are presented, explanations are absent or limited.
1	The response is very short, does not show full understanding of the question or prompt, and is hard for the listener to understand.	At least two (2) of these problems: poor pronunciation is used, speech is choppy (not fluent), there are long or frequent pauses, poor grammar use makes ideas difficult to understand, obviously practiced or formulaic expressions are used, there is lots of repetition of expressions in the prompt.
0	There is no response or the response is not related to the question or prompt.	There is no response to grade, or the response is not related to the question or prompt.

Test management

- You will speak into a microphone attached to a headset.
- Before you begin the speaking section, listen to the headset directions. It is very important that your microphone is working and that your voice can be heard clearly. It is also important that you can hear clearly during the listening section.
- Be aware of time constraints. Check the time with the clock shown in the title bar.
- Independent speaking questions come first.
- Note-taking is permitted. Paper will be provided by the test supervisor. These notes can be studied when preparing your response.
- If you miss something that is said in a conversation or lecture, do not panic. Forget about it, and simply keep listening. Even native speakers do not hear everything that is said.
- You must answer each question as it appears. You can NOT return to any questions later.
- Do not leave any question unanswered. You are NOT penalized for guessing an answer.

Introduction to the *Basic Skills for the TOEFL® iBT* series

Basic Skills for the TOEFL® iBT is a 3-level, 12-book test preparation series designed for beginning-level students of the TOEFL® iBT. Over the course of the series, students build on their current vocabulary to include common TOEFL® and academic vocabulary. They are also introduced to the innovative questions types found on the TOEFL® iBT, and are provided with practice of TOEFL® iBT reading, listening, speaking, and writing passages, conversations, lectures, and questions accessible to students of their level.

Basic Skills for the TOEFL® iBT enables students to build on both their language skills and their knowledge. The themes of the passages, lectures, and questions cover topics often seen on the TOEFL® iBT. In addition, the independent topics, while taking place in a university setting, are also accessible to and understood by students preparing to enter university. The academic topics are also ones that native speakers study.

Students accumulate vocabulary over the series. Vocabulary learned at the beginning of the series will appear in passages and lectures later in the book, level, and series. Each level gets progressively harder. The vocabulary becomes more difficult, the number of vocabulary words to be learned increases, and the passages, conversations, and lectures get longer and increase in level. By the end of the series, students will know all 570 words on the standard Academic Word List (AWL) used by TESOL and have a solid foundation in and understanding of the TOEFL® iBT.

Not only will *Basic Skills for the TOEFL® iBT* start preparing students for the TOEFL® iBT, but it will also give students a well-rounded basis for either further academic study in English or further TOEFL® iBT study.

Introduction to the *Basic Skills for the TOEFL® iBT* Speaking Book

This is the second speaking book in the *Basic Skills for the TOEFL® iBT* series. Each unit focuses on a different integrated question.

Units	Integrated Question	Content
1, 5, 9	Q3	Announcement and student conversation
2, 6, 10	Q4	Reading passage and lecture
3, 7, 11	Q5	Student conversation
4, 8, 12	Q6	Lecture

The academic passages and lectures will be on the topics that the student was introduced to in the Level 2 reading book. The passages, conversations, and lectures in Speaking Level 2 are longer and at a higher level, the questions are slightly more difficult, and there are more vocabulary words compared to Speaking Level 1.

Each unit is separated into 7 sections:

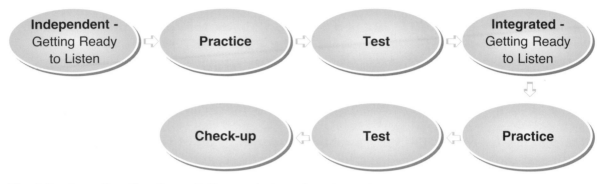

The following will outline the activities and aims of each section.

Key Vocabulary and TOEFL® Vocabulary

Students begin by studying the vocabulary they will encounter in the following section. **TOEFL® Vocabulary** includes the words that have been found to appear most often in TOEFL® preparation materials or are Academic Word List (AWL) words. TOEFL® Vocabulary includes the most important words for the student to learn in order to build his or her vocabulary before further TOEFL® study. **Key Vocabulary** includes the other words that are important for the student to know in order to understand the conversation that will follow.

Prompt

In this part, students are asked some simple questions about an experience in their own lives. This introduces students to the theme of the independent section and gets students talking about things with which they are familiar.

Practice

Prompt 1

Students ask each other questions about another experience in their own lives and then make a list of descriptive words that fit in with the prompt and that will be useful later for the test section.

Prompt 2

Students write answers to another aspect of the independent section's theme and then tell their answers to a partner. They then make another list of descriptive words that will be useful for the test section.

Prompt 3

Students are now introduced to the main prompt that will also be used in the test section and are given a list of words or phrases that will be useful for the test section.

Sample Response and Outline

Students will listen to two sample responses to the prompt and will fill out the outlines for them. This will enable students to hear the structure a response should take, and give them ideas for their own response in the test section. They will also get practice on how they can prepare for their own response using an outline. These responses will use all the vocabulary words studied at the beginning of the unit.

TOEFL® Vocabulary Practice

The next part contains sentences using the TOEFL® vocabulary the student learned at the beginning of the section. This helps students practice the words in context.

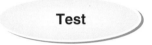

The test contains the same prompt that the students were introduced to in the practice section. They will now have the opportunity to create their own response.

The test is split into three steps and an extension. The first step allows the student to read the prompt as would happen in the real TOEFL® test. The second step then enables the student to prepare his or her response and in the third step students are given the opportunity to write out their responses to make them easier for the teacher to evaluate. The extension activity enables students to then practice responding to the prompt with three partners, and to time one another.

The answer key gives two further responses, which use many of the vocabulary words learned at the beginning of the section.

The integrated section varies depending on which TOEFL® question it is focusing on. This section will therefore identify which unit is being described.

Key Vocabulary and TOEFL® Vocabulary

This contains the Key Vocabulary and TOEFL® Vocabulary students will encounter in the following section. See the independent description for further details.

Units 1, 2, 5, 6, 9, and 10
Reading

In these units, students will be asked to read an announcement or reading passage. They are then asked two questions about what they have just read and one question about what they think the conversation/lecture will be about. The aim is to introduce the students to the theme of the integrated section.

Units 3, 4, 7, 8, 11, and 12
Listening

In these units, students will be asked to listen to the first part of a conversation or lecture. They are then asked two questions about what they have just heard and one question about what they think the rest of the conversation/lecture will be about. The aim is to introduce the students to the theme of the integrated section.

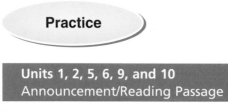

Practice

Units 1, 2, 5, 6, 9, and 10
Announcement/Reading Passage

Students read the announcement/reading passage again and underline the key information.

Note-taking

Students now listen to the corresponding conversation or lecture. The reading and listening together contain all the vocabulary words learned at the beginning of the integrated section.

Students take notes as they listen. The notes are guided so that the student can fill in the parts that are missing.

Prompt

Students are now given the prompt to which they need to respond.

Units 3, 4, 7, 8, 11, and 12
Note-taking

Students now listen to the full conversation or lecture. The listening contains all the vocabulary words learned at the beginning of the integrated section.

Students take notes as they listen. The notes are guided so that the student can fill in the parts that are missing.

The student is then asked to answer further questions about the listening. This helps the student prepare for his or her response.

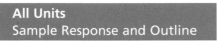

Prompt

Students are now given the prompt to which they need to respond.

All Units
Sample Response and Outline

The students now listen to a sample response and complete the outline for it. This will enable students to hear the structure a response should take and practice how they can prepare for their own response with an outline.

Speaking Practice

Students should now practice saying a response using the information in the completed outline.

TOEFL® Vocabulary Practice

The next part contains sentences using the TOEFL® vocabulary the student learned at the beginning of the integrated section. This helps students practice the words in context.

Test

Units 1, 2, 5, 6, 9, and 10

In these units, the test is split into five steps and an extension. In **step one**, students read the announcement/passage. In **step two**, they listen to the conversation/lecture and complete the notes. In **step three**, they read the prompt. In **step four**, they complete an outline for their response. In **step five**, they write out a full response and in the extension, they practice their response with three partners, and time one another.

Units 3, 4, 7, 8, 11, and 12

In these units, the test is split into four steps and an extension. In **step one**, students listen to the conversation/lecture and complete the notes. In **step two**, they read the prompt. In **step three**, they complete an outline for their response. In **step four**, they write out a full response and in the extension they practice their response with three partners, and time one another.

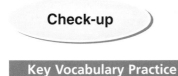

Check-up

Key Vocabulary Practice

This part is sentences using the Key vocabulary the student learned over the course of the unit. This helps students practice the words in context.

Sample Speaking Lesson Plan - 50 minutes

Homework Check	5 min.	• Check that students completed their homework and talk about any problems they had.
Review	5 min.	• Review the strategies discussed in the previous unit and talk about other strategies students might have employed when they did homework. • Compare the answers different students gave in their homework and ask some students to speak in front of the class while the rest of the class is split into groups and evaluates them using the form at the back of the book. All students should have to speak in front of the class at least once over the course of the book.

Main Lesson	35 min.	✳ Students often find the independent sections easier, so these could be completed for homework. The independent and integrated sections may also be alternately taught in the classroom.
		
		Integrated - Getting Ready to Speak (Unit 1 used as an example)
		A. Learn the words
		  • Preview the vocabulary and have students read the words aloud.
		  • Talk about what parts of speech the words belong to.
		B. Read/Listen
		  • Have the students read and then answer the questions with a partner.
		  • As a class, predict what the conversation will be about.
		
		Practice
		A. Announcement
		  • Read the announcement again, this time as a class. Try to identify the most important information in it.
		B. Note-taking
		  • Have students listen to the conversation and take notes.
		  • Ask students to compare their notes with a classmate and ensure they all have the main information. Emphasize that each student's notes may be written differently, but that they should all include the same main points.
		C. Prompt
		  • Read the prompt as a class and discuss the meaning of it. Ensure that all students have the same understanding of the prompt.
		D. Sample response and outline
		  • Put students into groups and play the sample response. You may need to play it two or three times. The group should then have a completed outline.
		  • Compare each group's outline and ensure that each has the correct information.
		E. Speaking practice
		  • Have each student in the group take turns saying the response by following the same completed outline. Emphasize that each response should include the same information but that sentences and vocabulary may differ.
		F. TOEFL vocabulary practice
		  • Ask students to complete the sentences and check their answers in pairs.
		
		Test
		  • Students should complete the test individually.
		  • Compare outlines and practice the response with a partner. They should evaluate each other using the form at the back of the book.
		
		Independent - Getting Ready to Speak (Next unit)
		A. Learn the words
		  • Preview the vocabulary and have students read the words aloud.
		  • Talk about what parts of speech the words belong to.
		B. Read the prompt
		  • Students should read the prompt and answer the related questions with a partner.
		  • Students could also ask each other further questions related to the prompt.
		  • Have students listen to the sample and repeat it.

Wrap-up	5 min.	• Give homework (the rest of the independent section.) ✳ The Integrated test and the check-up can also be given as homework.

Teaching Tips

- It is strongly recommended that the class go through the target vocabulary prior to starting the rest of the unit.

- It is a good idea to have students make their own vocabulary lists on their PCs or in their notebooks. Putting the words under thematic categories (categories of subjects) would be an effective way to study the words.

- It is important to emphasize an understanding of the main idea of the conversations and lectures. Students often listen without constructing the framework, which could cause them problems in understanding the main points and how they relate to the announcement/passage and the prompt.

- The first class should take time to introduce the outline format. Then, when students are asked to use the outlines later, they are familiar and therefore not as intimidating.

- Note-taking practice needs to be done in class with the teacher's assistance in the beginning because not many students are familiar with note-taking. Gradually, have students take notes in groups, pairs, and then individually.

- Timing students' responses is an effective activity. Teachers can give a target length of time and increase it over the course of the book or series.

- Encourage students to do timed-activities even when they do their homework.

- If students have access to recording devices, then it is good practice to record themselves giving their response and listen to it again, noting where they think they could improve and how long their response is.

- Students can use the definitions and synonyms in the vocabulary section when they give their responses.

- Use the test at the end of each unit as a progress check. Students' responses should become more organized and longer as the book and series progresses.

[01] Independent

Getting Ready to Speak

A. Learn the words.

Key Vocabulary

Jewish	following or related to the religion of Judaism
hardship	a difficulty
hope	to want or expect something
cultural	relating to arts or other intellectual activity

TOEFL Vocabulary

specific	precise; exact
endure	to tolerate something
overcome	to conquer or defeat a problem
accomplish	to achieve something
authentic	real

B. Read the prompt. Then answer the questions.

Talk about your favorite movie.

1. What is your favorite movie?
My favorite movie is _____.

2. When did you first see this movie?
I first saw this movie _____.

3. Why do you like this movie so much?
I like this movie because _____.

Now practice the questions and answers with a partner.

C. Listen and repeat. Track 1

Practice

A. Read the prompt. Then take turns answering the questions with a partner.

Talk about the most recent book that you have read.

1. What book did you read?
2. Did you enjoy the book? Why or why not?
3. What important things did the book teach you?
4. Would you recommend this book to others? Why?

B. Make a list of descriptive words and phrases to describe books with your classmates.

_____

_____

_____

_____

C. Read the prompt. Then complete the answers with your own information.

Talk about a positive message from a book or movie that you have seen.

Which?   The book/movie _____ taught me a very positive message.

What?   It taught me to _____.

How?   It showed this message by _____.

Why?   This message is important because _____

_____.

Now practice your answers with a partner.

D. Make a list of positive description words and phrases with a partner.

_____

_____

_____

_____

E. Read the prompt. Then underline the phrases you could use in your own response.

> Describe a movie or book that has had a positive influence on you. Include specific details and examples in your response.

How the movie changed you

- made me think in a new way
- helped me realize . . .
- opened my eyes to . . .
- made me act a new way
- made me start a new habit
- helped me to understand

Sample Response and Outline

F. Listen to the sample responses and complete the outlines. Track 2

Sample response 1

(_____)

What happened	How it influenced me
_____	_____
_____	_____
_____	_____
_____	_____

Conclusion: _____

Sample response 2

(_____)

What happened	How it influenced me
_____	_____
_____	_____
_____	_____
_____	_____

Conclusion: _____

TOEFL Vocabulary Practice

G. Fill in the blanks with the correct words.

| specific | endure | overcome | accomplished | authentic |

1. It can sometimes be difficult to see if a painting is _____ or fake.
2. Many people like math more than history because math always has a _____ answer.
3. Helen Keller was able to _____ being deaf and blind, and eventually learned to communicate.
4. Soldiers taken during war often have to _____ a lot of pain.
5. In 1969, the United States _____ its goal of putting a man on the moon.

Test

Step 1

Read the prompt.

> Describe a movie or book that has had a positive influence on you. Include specific details and examples in your response.

Step 2

Create an outline for your response.

_____

What happened

_____

_____

_____

_____

Conclusion: _____

_____

How it influenced you

_____

_____

_____

_____

Step 3

Write a response using your outline from above.

The _____ had a very positive influence on my life.

It is about _____

_____.

It taught me _____

_____.

I hope _____

_____.

Extension

👤👤 **Work with a partner. Take turns saying your response. Then change partners two more times. Time yourselves!**

Your time: _____ seconds   Partner one's time: _____ seconds

Your time: _____ seconds   Partner two's time: _____ seconds

Your time: _____ seconds   Partner three's time: _____ seconds

Getting Ready to Speak

A. Learn the words.

Key Vocabulary

bus system	an organized network of routes for transportation by bus
enough	as much as is needed; adequate
bus stop	a specific location where a bus stops to pick up and let off passengers
apartment	a place of residence situated with other similar units in a larger building

TOEFL Vocabulary

route	a road, way, or path that is traveled
no longer	not now; not anymore
inconvenience	the state of being caused bother, trouble, or difficulty
repair	to fix or mend; to restore to a good condition
expensive	highly priced; costly

B. Read the announcement. Then answer the questions.

Change of Bus Route

The university bus system will change one bus route. In the past, buses have stopped in front of SaveMart on Preston Road. However, not enough students use the Preston Road bus route. The university will no longer run buses to Preston Road. Students using the Preston Road bus stop should begin using the Davis Boulevard stop a half kilometer to the south of the old Preston Road bus stop. We are sorry for any inconvenience this may cause students.

1. What will happen?
Buses will not _____.

2. What should students do?
Students should _____.

3. What do you think the conversation will be about?
I think the conversation will be about _____
_____.

Now practice the questions and answers with a partner.

C. Listen and repeat. Track 3

Practice

A. Read the announcement again and underline the key information.

> ### Change of Bus Route
>
> The university bus system will change one bus route. In the past, buses have stopped in front of SaveMart on Preston Road. However, not enough students use the Preston Road bus route. The university will no longer run buses to Preston Road. Students using the Preston Road bus stop should begin using the Davis Boulevard stop a half kilometer to the south of the old Preston Road bus stop. We are sorry for any inconvenience this may cause students.

Note-taking

B. Listen to the conversation and take notes. `Track 4`

Man	Woman
• The school is _____ _____ • Take the bus to _____ _____ • Walk to _____ • The university doesn't have _____ _____ _____	• Not happy about _____ • Used bus route to _____ _____ • It will be _____ _____ • The university should spend less on _____ _____

Prompt

C. Read the prompt.

> The woman and man express their opinions about the announcement made by the university bus service. State their opinions and explain the reasons they give for holding those opinions.

D. Listen to the sample response and complete the outline. `Track 5`

The woman is not happy about _____.

   A. It is an inconvenience

      1. to take the _____

      2. to have to shop _____ _____

   B. The man

      1. doesn't think _____

      2. thinks the university doesn't _____

E. Now work with a partner. Take turns saying your own response using the outline from above.

Your time: _____ seconds   Your partner's time: _____ seconds

F. Fill in the blanks with the correct words.

expensive   inconvenience   route   no longer   repairing

1. When a road is closed, people have to take a different _____.

2. People _____ believe the world is flat.

3. Buying a brand-new computer is _____.

4. _____ a car often costs a lot of money.

5. It is an _____ for the main road to a school to be closed.

Test

Step 1

Read the announcement.

> **Road Closing**
>
> Starting next week, Kirby Road will be closed from University Drive to Main Street. The city will be working on repairs to Kirby Road for the fall semester. All students who walk to classes along this route will need to find another way to get to classes. The large trucks and machines used for road repairs will make walking along Kirby Road dangerous. Therefore, police will not allow students access to the area while the road is being repaired.

Step 2

Listen to the conversation and take notes. `Track 6`

Woman	Man
• Asks if man knows that the _____ _____	• Going to make walk to _____ _____
• Will have to leave at least _____ _____	• Thinks the road needs _____ _____
• The road had _____ _____	_____
• Thinks they did the right thing by _____	

Step 3

Read the prompt.

> The man and woman express their opinions of the announcement made about the road closing. State their opinions and explain the reasons they give for holding those opinions.

Step 4

Create an outline for your response.

The man is not happy about _____.

    A. The man

        1. is going to have to _____

        2. thinks the road should be repaired but should let students _____

        _____

    B. The woman

        1. will need to leave earlier to get to _____

        2. thinks the road _____

        3. thinks it could be _____

Step 5

Write a response using your outline from above.

>   The man _____
> because he is going to have to _____.
> He also thinks the road should be repaired but _____
> _____.
> The woman will need to leave her _____.
> She thinks the road needs repair but also thinks _____
> _____.

Extension

Work with a partner. Take turns saying your response. Then change partners two more times. Time yourselves!

Your time: _____ seconds   Partner one's time: _____ seconds

Your time: _____ seconds   Partner two's time: _____ seconds

Your time: _____ seconds   Partner three's time: _____ seconds

Check-up

Fill in the blanks with the correct words.

bus stop	enough	apartment	bus system
Jewish	hardships	hope	cultural

1. In an _____ building, there are many residential units.
2. Students often do not have _____ money to pay for expensive things.
3. It is helpful to have a _____ near one's house.
4. Some cities have no subways so people have to use the _____.
5. There are many _____ differences between Asians and Westerners.
6. Israel is the only _____ country in the world.
7. All parents _____ that their children have happy lives.
8. During wars, people experience many terrible _____.

[02] Independent

Getting Ready to Speak

A. Learn the words.

Key Vocabulary

career	a long-term job
salary	the amount of money paid to a worker
rent	the payment to live in a home
emotional	affected by feelings

TOEFL Vocabulary

sufficient	enough
ensure	to make sure
creative	new and original
satisfy	to fulfill a need
duty	a responsibility

B. Read the prompt. Then answer the questions.

Talk about your mother's or father's job.

1. What does your mother or father do?
   My mother/father is a _____.

2. Where does your mother/father work?
   She/He works _____.

3. How long has he worked there?
   She/He has worked there _____.

Now practice the questions and answers with a partner.

C. Listen and repeat. Track 7

Practice

Prompt 1

A. Read the prompt. Then take turns answering the questions with a partner.

> **What do you think is the perfect job? Explain.**

1. What do you think is the perfect job?
2. Do you know anyone with this job? Who?
3. What is your favorite thing about the job?
4. Why is this job perfect?

B. Make a list of interesting jobs with your classmates.

_____

_____

_____

_____

Prompt 2

C. Read the prompt. Then complete the answers with your own information.

> **Talk about someone you know who is happy with his or her career.**

Who? _____ is really happy with his/her career.

What? He/She works as a _____.

When? He/She started working at his/her job _____.

Why? He/She loves his/her job because _____.

Now practice your answers with a partner.

D. Make a list of reasons to have a great job with a partner.

_____

_____

_____

_____

E. Read the prompt. Then underline the phrases you could use in your own answer.

What do you think is the most important thing when you are choosing a career? Include specific details and examples in your response.

Important things when choosing a career

- doing something interesting
- high status
- be satisfied with my job
- allowed to be creative
- making a lot of money
- respect of others

Sample Response and Outline

F. Listen to the sample responses and complete the outlines. Track 8

Sample response 1

_____

Reason 1	Reason 2
_____	_____
Support _____	Support _____
_____	_____
_____	_____

Conclusion: _____

Sample response 2

_____

Reason 1	Reason 2
_____	_____
Support _____	Support _____
_____	_____
_____	_____

Conclusion: _____

TOEFL Vocabulary Practice

G. Fill in the blanks with the correct words.

sufficient	ensure	creative	satisfied	duty

1. Even though a Mercedes Benz is expensive, its owner is usually _____ with the car.

2. It is a judge's _____ to always be fair and honest.

3. Being friendly with others will _____ that you are never lonely.

4. Most people think that artists and singers are _____ people.

5. Millions of poor people in Africa do not have a _____ amount of food.

Test

Step 1

Read the prompt.

> What do you think is the most important thing when you are choosing a career?
> Include specific details and examples in your response.

Step 2

Create an outline for your response.

_____

Reason 1

_____

_____

Support _____

_____

_____

Conclusion: _____

_____

Reason 2

_____

_____

Support _____

_____

_____

Step 3

Write a response using your outline from above.

> The most important thing when choosing a career is _____
>
> _____.
>
> This is important because _____
>
> _____.
>
> In addition, _____
>
> _____.
>
> _____ is important when choosing a career.

👤👤 **Work with a partner. Take turns saying your response. Then change partners two more times. Time yourselves!**

Your time: _____ seconds	Partner one's time: _____ seconds
Your time: _____ seconds	Partner two's time: _____ seconds
Your time: _____ seconds	Partner three's time: _____ seconds

Integrated

Getting Ready to Speak

A. Learn the words.

stainless steel	a type of metal that does not rust
curve	a line that gradually bends like part of a circle
movement	an effort by a large group of people to try to change something
sunburst	a burst of sunlight

technical	requiring specialized knowledge or ability, especially in math or science
diverse	made up of many differing parts
worldwide	all over the world
interior	the inside of a building, especially the way it is decorated
disposal	the power to use something

B. Read the passage. Then answer the questions.

Art Deco Architecture

Architecture became more technical in the twentieth century. This meant that buildings could be taller. These new very tall buildings were called skyscrapers. The first ones were in America. One of the most popular styles of design in the 1920s was Art Deco. Its influences were diverse. It could be seen on the buildings and inside them too. Many buildings were made with stainless steel and glass. They often had large spires and big curves. This style can be seen on the Chrysler building in New York.

1. What was one of the most popular styles of design in the 1920s?
   One of the most popular styles of design in the 1920s was _____.

2. What were many Art Deco buildings built with?
   Many Art Deco buildings were built with _____.

3. What do you think the lecture will be about?
   I think that the lecture will be about _____.

👤👤 **Now practice the questions and answers with a partner.**

🎧 **C. Listen and repeat.** Track 9

Practice

A. Read the passage again and underline the key information.

> ### Art Deco Architecture
> Architecture became more technical in the twentieth century. This meant that buildings could be taller. These new very tall buildings were called skyscrapers. The first ones were in America. One of the most popular styles of design in the 1920s was Art Deco. Its influences were diverse. It could be seen on the buildings and inside them too. Many buildings were made with stainless steel and glass. They often had large spires and big curves. This style can be seen on the Chrysler building in New York.

Note-taking

B. Listen to the lecture and take notes. Track 10

Art Deco

- Was a very popular _____
- It can still be seen _____

Art Deco Designers

- Used modern _____
- Were inspired by _____

The style

- Was all about _____
- Used many _____
- Could be found _____
- Is still _____

The Chrysler Building

- Had a _____
- Was made using _____

Prompt

C. Read the prompt.

> The professor and the passage give details about Art Deco. Explain what Art Deco was like and where it was used.

D. Listen to the sample response and complete the outline. `Track 11`

The lecture and the passage were about _____.

A. Art Deco was a

   1. popular _____

   2. very modern _____

B. The style was

   1. about making _____

   2. used in _____

C. Art Deco buildings

   1. often had _____

   2. were made _____

All of these things can be seen _____.

E. Now work with a partner. Take turns saying your own response using the outline from above.

Your time: _____ seconds   Your partner's time: _____ seconds

F. Fill in the blanks with the correct words.

technical	diverse	worldwide	interior	disposal

1. If a movie is popular all over the world, someone could say it was successful _____.

2. If a person buys a box of candy bars, it could be said that they have a lot of them at their _____.

3. A city where people from very different places live would be called culturally _____.

4. When something electrical breaks, it is often because of a _____ fault.

5. When people move into an old house, they often want to change the _____ design.

Test

Step 1

Read the passage.

> ### The Empire State Building
>
> The Empire State building is the tallest skyscraper in New York. It is an Art Deco building. It was built in 1930, toward the end of the Art Deco movement. It was the tallest building in the world for over forty years. It is very famous worldwide. It was made using limestone and stainless steel. It rises in a series of setbacks like a pyramid. This Egyptian style was a common theme of Art Deco.

Step 2

Listen to the lecture and take notes. Track 12

The Empire State Building

- Is one of the _____
- Has appeared _____
- Looks like _____
- Was built in _____
- Took sixteen months to build because _____

The Building's Art Deco Style

- Is unlike _____
- It does not have _____
- The top has a _____
- It is like a _____

The Art Deco Movement

- Was influenced by _____
- Mixed _____

Step 3

Read the prompt.

The professor and the passage talk about the Empire State building. Explain how the building mixes old and new styles to become famous.

Step 4

Create an outline for your response.

The passage and lecture were about _____.
    A. The Empire State building
        1. is the tallest _____
        2. is one of the _____ _____
    B. Was built using _____
    C. Looks like it _____
    D. Built quickly because _____
    E. On top it has _____
    F. The style was influenced _____

Step 5

Write a response using your outline from above.

The passage and lecture were _____.
It was built _____ and it is the _____.
It is one of the best-known _____ in the world.
It was built using _____.
The building looks like it has _____.
It was built in only sixteen months because of _____.
It has an _____. Designers used this
style because _____.

Extension

Work with a partner. Take turns saying your response. Then change partners two more times. Time yourselves!

Your time: _____ seconds   Partner one's time: _____ seconds
Your time: _____ seconds   Partner two's time: _____ seconds
Your time: _____ seconds   Partner three's time: _____ seconds

Check-up

Fill in the blanks with the correct words.

stainless steel	curve	movement	sunburst
career	salary	rent	emotional

1. Art Deco was a popular design _____ of the 1920s.
2. When the Sun first comes up in the morning, you can see a _____.
3. _____ is used to make cutlery because it does not rust.
4. When driving around hills, there could be more than one _____ in the road.
5. University students often think it is difficult to choose a _____.
6. _____ in big cities is much higher than in small cities because there isn't as much space.
7. Doctors earn a much higher _____ than teachers.
8. Parents are often very _____ when they watch their children graduate.

[03] Independent

Getting Ready to Speak

A. Learn the words.

Key Vocabulary

invention	something new that is created
plastic	a synthetic material
depend	to rely on somebody or something
journey	a trip somewhere

TOEFL Vocabulary

profound	great
traditional	relating to an old custom or belief
versatile	having many uses
superior	better than others
crucial	important

B. Read the prompt. Then answer the questions.

> Talk about something that you use every day.

1. What do you use?
Every day I use _____.

2. How often do you use this?
I use it _____.

3. How does this help you?
It helps me _____.

Now practice the questions and answers with a partner.

C. Listen and repeat. Track 13

Practice

A. Read the prompt. Then take turns answering the questions with a partner.

Talk about what invention you would make to help everyone in the world.

1. What would you call your invention?
2. What would your invention do?
3. Why do you want to invent this?
4. How will this invention help other people?

B. Make a list of inventions and what they do with your classmates.

_____

_____

_____

_____

Prompt 2

C. Read the prompt. Then complete the answers with your own information.

Talk about the invention of the computer.

What?   The computer lets us _____.

Where?   Now, we can use computers _____.

How?   Computers have changed our lives because _____

_____.

Why?   Computers are important because _____

_____.

Now practice your answers with a partner.

D. Make a list of things that you wish there was an invention for with a partner.

_____

_____

_____

_____

E. Read the prompt. Then underline the phrases you could use in your own answer.

What do you think has been the greatest invention to date? Include specific details and examples in your response.

Reasons for liking an invention

- helped to understand better
- superior design
- made our lives easier
- gave more people access
- saved many people's lives
- more versatile

Sample Response and Outline

F. Listen to the sample responses and complete the outlines. `Track 14`

Sample response 1		Sample response 2	
_____		_____	
Reason 1	**Reason 2**	**Reason 1**	**Reason 2**
_____	_____	_____	_____
_____	_____	_____	_____
Support _____	**Support** _____	**Support** _____	**Support** _____
_____	_____	_____	_____
_____	_____	_____	_____
Conclusion: _____		**Conclusion:** _____	
_____		_____	

TOEFL Vocabulary Practice

G. Fill in the blanks with the correct words.

profound   traditional   versatile   superior   crucial

1. Many people in Asia prefer _____ medicine rather than modern Western medicine.
2. Duct tape is so _____. You can use it to fix anything.
3. Mohandas Gandhi had a _____ impact on many people including Martin Luther King Jr.
4. To be successful in business, it is _____ that you provide good service.
5. Paying more for clothes usually means that you get _____ quality and design.

Test

Step 1

Read the prompt.

What do you think has been the greatest invention to date? Include specific details and examples in your response.

Step 2

Create an outline for your response.

_____

Reason 1

_____

_____

Support _____

_____

Conclusion: _____

_____

Reason 2

_____

_____

Support _____

_____

Step 3

Write a response using your outline from above.

_____ is the greatest invention. It is crucial because

_____

_____.

It also _____

_____

_____.

_____ is the greatest invention of them all.

Extension

Work with a partner. Take turns saying your response. Then change partners two more times. Time yourselves!

Your time: _____ seconds   Partner one's time: _____ seconds

Your time: _____ seconds   Partner two's time: _____ seconds

Your time: _____ seconds   Partner three's time: _____ seconds

Integrated

Getting Ready to Speak

A. Learn the words.

shame	an unfortunate incident
innocent	not guilty
expel	to officially force someone to leave a school or an organization
kick out	to remove or eject someone from a program or a place

accuse	to claim that someone has done something, usually bad
policy	a standard agreed way of doing something
plagiarism	the act of copying another person's work and claiming it as your own
deceive	to trick
resort	to choose an unfavorable option

B. Listen to the first part of a conversation. Then answer the questions. `Track 15`

1. What are the students discussing?
   The students are discussing _____.

2. What did she see?
   The student saw _____.

3. What do you think the rest of the conversation will be about?
   I think the rest of the conversation will be about _____.

4. What do you think the woman should do?
   I think the woman should _____.

Now practice the questions and answers with a partner.

C. Listen and repeat. `Track 16`

Practice

A. **Listen to the full conversation and take notes.** `Track 17`

Reasons to tell her professor	Reasons not to tell her professor
• Saw _____ • The university's policy _____ _____ • Cheating is _____ • Telling her professor is _____ _____ • He _____ and should be _____ • It's not _____ _____	• What if he's _____ • Students who cheat are _____ _____ • Maybe he's _____ _____

B. **Use your notes to complete the answers.**

1. What are some of the reasons the students discuss for telling the professor?

   The students discuss _____
   _____.

2. What are some of the reasons the student shouldn't tell her professor?

   The student shouldn't tell her professor because _____
   _____.

Now practice the questions and answers with a partner.

C. **Read the prompt.**

> The students discuss whether the student should tell her professor about the other student cheating or not. Describe the reasons for each choice. Then state which you think is the better option.

D. Listen to the sample response and complete the outline. Track 18

The conversation is about _____.

A. Reasons for telling her professor

1. Cheating is _____

2. It's not _____ _____

3. The student should be _____

B. Reasons for not telling her professor

1. Doesn't want to _____

2. Maybe he had _____

    • Too busy with _____

    • Personal _____

Conclusion: She should be more understanding of him and _____
_____.

E. Write your own conclusion using the outline from above.

Conclusion: I think _____

because _____.

F. Now work with a partner. Take turns saying your own response using the outline from above.

Your time: _____ seconds   Your partner's time: _____ seconds

G. Fill in the blanks with the correct words.

accuse   deceive   plagiarism   policy   resort

1. You shouldn't _____ someone of a crime if you don't have any proof.

2. _____ is a big problem in many universities.

3. What is your country's _____ on capital punishment?

4. It's unfortunate when people have to _____ to stealing to get food.

5. Children often _____ their parents when they want something.

Test

Step 1

Listen to the conversation and take notes. `Track 19`

Woman	Man
• Wants to _____ _____	• Is worried about _____ _____
• Won't _____ _____	• Doesn't want to _____ _____
• Doesn't have _____ _____	• Needs to _____ _____
• Will give _____ _____	

Step 2

Read the prompt.

> The students are discussing sharing the man's essay. Discuss the man's and the woman's ideas about helping each other. Then, state if you would share your essay with the woman and why.

Step 3

Create an outline for your response.

The conversation is about _____.

    A. The woman

       1. wants to _____

       2. doesn't have time to _____

       3. will give _____

    B. The man

       1. is worried about _____

       2. doesn't want to _____

       3. needs to _____

Conclusion: I would _____.

Step 4

Write a response using your outline.

The conversation is about _____.

The woman wants to _____ because

_____.

She will _____.

However, the problems with sharing an essay are _____

_____.

If I were the man, I would _____

_____.

Work with a partner. Take turns saying your response. Then change partners two more times. Time yourselves!

Your time: _____ seconds   Partner one's time: _____ seconds

Your time: _____ seconds   Partner two's time: _____ seconds

Your time: _____ seconds   Partner three's time: _____ seconds

Check-up

Fill in the blanks with the correct words.

expelled	innocent	kick out	shame
invention	plastic	journey	depends

1. At a trial, a person is found guilty or _____.
2. Some parents _____ their children when they finish university.
3. It's a _____ when natural disasters happen.
4. Students who break a school's rules may be _____.
5. Magellan was the first person to _____ around the world.
6. Your taste in music often _____ on your personality.
7. People used to use feathers for pens; now, almost all pens are _____.
8. The _____ of penicillin helped to save thousands of lives.

[04] Independent

Getting Ready to Speak

A. Learn the words.

Key Vocabulary

respect	to admire and value someone else
wisdom	accumulated knowledge from life experience
lead	to guide someone
rid	to free yourself of something

TOEFL Vocabulary

diligent	hard-working
neglect	to ignore someone or something
charity	the giving of one's free time, money, or goods to people who need help
welfare	well-being
simultaneously	at the same time

B. Read the prompt. Then answer the questions.

Talk about a family member who you respect.

1. Which family member do you respect?
   I respect my _____.

2. Why do you respect him or her?
   I respect my _____ because _____
   _____.

3. Do you want to be like this family member? Why or why not?
   I want/don't want to be like my _____ because _____
   _____.

Now practice the questions and answers with a partner.

C. **Listen and repeat.** Track 20

Practice

Prompt 1

A. Read the prompt. Then take turns answering the questions with a partner.

Talk about someone you know who helps make lives better.

1. Who do you know that makes others' lives better?
2. What does he/she do?
3. How often does he/she do this?
4. How does he/she help to make others' lives better?

B. Make a list of ways to help other people with your classmates.

_____

_____

_____

_____

Prompt 2

C. Read the prompt. Then complete the answers with your own information.

Talk about your favorite athlete, singer, or movie star.

Who?   My favorite athlete/singer/movie star is _____.

What?   He/She _____.

When?   I started watching him/her when _____.

Why?   He/She is my favorite athlete/singer/movie star because _____

_____.

Now practice your answers with a partner.

D. Make a list of famous people who you respect with a partner.

_____

_____

_____

_____

E. Read the prompt. Then underline the phrases you could use in your own answer.

Describe the person you respect the most. Include specific details and examples in your response.

Reasons why you respect people

- they are diligent
- they have a lot of wisdom
- they give time to charity

- they lead others well
- they care about others' welfare
- they respect everyone

F. Listen to the sample responses and complete the outlines. Track 21

Sample response 1

_____

Reason 1	Reason 2
_____	_____
Support _____	Support _____
_____	_____
_____	_____

Conclusion: _____

Sample response 2

_____

Reason 1	Reason 2
_____	_____
Support _____	Support _____
_____	_____
_____	_____

Conclusion: _____

G. Fill in the blanks with the correct words.

diligent   neglect   welfare   simultaneously   charity

1. Parents must always care for the _____ of their children.
2. To play the piano, you must use your right and left hands _____.
3. People often feel good after helping out a _____.
4. _____ students usually get good grades.
5. People who _____ their health usually feel sick more often than people who take care of themselves.

Test

Step 1

Read the prompt.

Describe the person you respect the most. Include specific details and examples in your response.

Step 2

Create an outline for your response.

_____

Reason 1

_____

_____

Support _____

_____

_____

Reason 2

_____

_____

Support _____

_____

_____

Conclusion: _____

_____

Step 3

Write a response using your outline from above.

I respect _____ more than anyone else.

I respect _____ because _____

_____.

Simultaneously, he/she _____

_____.

I think _____ is a great man/woman.

Extension

Work with a partner. Take turns saying your response. Then change partners two more times. Time yourselves!

Your time: _____ seconds   Partner one's time: _____ seconds

Your time: _____ seconds   Partner two's time: _____ seconds

Your time: _____ seconds   Partner three's time: _____ seconds

Integrated

Getting Ready to Speak

A. Learn the words.

Key Vocabulary

carnivore	an animal (or plant) that eats animals
snap	to close quickly
juice	a liquid that comes from a plant
digest	to process food

TOEFL Vocabulary

factor	something that has a big influence on something else
deficient	inadequate; not enough
series	a group of similar things that come one after another
stimulate	to cause a physical response
emit	to send or give out something

B. Listen to the first part of a lecture. Then answer the questions. `Track 22`

1. What is the lecture mainly about?
   It is about _____.

2. How is this plant different?
   It is different because _____.

3. Why do you think the plant has to do this?
   I think the plant has to do this because _____.

Now practice the questions and answers with a partner.

C. Listen and repeat. `Track 23`

Practice

Note-taking

A. Listen to the full lecture and take notes. Track 24

- Special plant
- Different because _____
- Called a _____
- They eat _____ because _____
- Eating insects _____
- Also need _____
- Leaves are _____
- When an insect stimulates the hairs it _____
- Plant emits _____ to _____
- Plant must be careful because _____

B. Use your notes to complete the answers.

1. What reasons does the professor give for the Venus Flytrap being a carnivore?

   The professor says that Venus Flytraps must be carnivores because _____

   _____.

2. Why does the professor say that the Venus Flytrap must be careful?

   The professor says that the Venus Flytrap must be careful because _____

   _____.

Now practice the questions and answers with a partner.

Prompt

C. Read the prompt.

> The professor talked about the Venus Flytrap. Using points and examples from the lecture, discuss how the Venus Flytrap is special among plants.

D. Listen to the sample response and complete the outline. `Track 25`

The lecture is about a _____ plant named the _____.

A. What it needs to live

    1. Insects: _____

       • Needs them because _____ _____

    2. Air and Water: _____

B. Leaves

    1. Shape: _____

    2. Each leaf has _____

C. When insects touch the leaf it _____

D. The plant _____

    1. This _____

    2. The plant then _____

E. Must be careful because _____

Conclusion: Venus Flytraps are _____.

E. Now work with a partner. Take turns saying your own response using the outline from above.

Your time: _____ seconds   Your partner's time: _____ seconds

F. Fill in the blanks with the correct words.

factor	deficient	series	stimulate	emits

1. A _____ of words together make a sentence.

2. The Sun _____ rays of sunshine.

3. Not exercising is a main _____ in people being overweight.

4. When a person is sleep _____, it is very difficult for them to concentrate and stay awake.

5. Restaurants often give bread to customers before the meal to _____ their appetite.

Test

Step 1

Listen to the lecture and take notes. Track 26

- All carnivore plants _____
- Different plants catch insects in different ways.
- The Venus Flytrap uses a _____
- When the leaf is stimulated, _____
- Another kind of plant catches insects with glue.
- When an insect touches the leaf, _____
- Lobster traps are usually found _____
- They work because _____
- Bowl-shaped plants emit _____
- The walls are high, so _____

Step 2

Read the prompt.

> The professor describes how carnivore plants catch insects. Using points and examples from the lecture, describe how these plants catch insects.

Step 3

Create an outline for your response.

The lecture is about how carnivore plants catch insects.

    A. Snap traps: Leaves snap shut when _____

    B. Insects that use glue

        1. Plants emit _____

        2. When insects _____

    C. Lobster Trap

        1. Usually found _____

        2. It's easy _____

        3. It's difficult _____

    D. Bowl-shaped plant

        1. Plant emits _____

        2. Insects want to _____

        3. The insects _____

Conclusion: Many ways _____.

Step 4

Write a response using your outline.

> This lecture is about _____.
> All carnivore plants are the same because _____
> _____.
> But they are different because _____.
> The snap trap plants _____.
> Other plants use glue. When insects touch _____.
> Lobster traps are easy _____, but _____
> _____.
> Bowl plants catch insects by _____.
> The insect then _____.

Extension

👤👤 **Work with a partner. Take turns saying your response. Then change partners two more times. Time yourselves!**

Your time: _____ seconds   Partner one's time: _____ seconds
Your time: _____ seconds   Partner two's time: _____ seconds
Your time: _____ seconds   Partner three's time: _____ seconds

Check-up

Fill in the blanks with the correct words.

carnivores	snap	juice	digest
respect	wisdom	leading	rid

1. People often say to wait an hour before going swimming to let your food _____.

2. You must be careful when using a mousetrap that it doesn't _____ your fingers.

3. Tyrannosaurus Rex was one of the most ferocious _____ of all time.

4. It is smart to drink the _____ from coconuts if you cannot find water.

5. Young people usually do not have much _____.

6. During the Cold War, both the US and Soviet Union had to _____ each other because they each had bombs.

7. In 1979, doctors were able to _____ the world of small pox, a very deadly disease.

8. Ghengis Khan died _____ his army to war.

[05] Independent

Getting Ready to Speak

A. Learn the words.

Key Vocabulary

holiday	a day to celebrate a special person or event, often connected to religion
celebration	an event to show happiness about something
pray	to speak to a god in order to ask for help or to give thanks
war	a long armed fight between groups or countries

TOEFL Vocabulary

ceremony	a ritual for a formal occasion
religion	a set of beliefs based on faith
national	associated with a country
honor	to respect
resist	to refuse to give in

B. Read the prompt. Then answer the questions.

Talk about the most recent holiday that you celebrated.

1. Which holiday did you celebrate?
   I recently celebrated _____.

2. What did you do that was special to celebrate that day?
   For _____, I _____.

3. Did you enjoy the holiday? Why?
   I enjoyed/didn't enjoy the holiday because _____
   _____.

Now practice the questions and answers with a partner.

C. Listen and repeat. Track 27

Practice

Prompt 1

A. Read the prompt. Then take turns answering the questions with a partner.

Talk about a religious holiday either you or your friend celebrates.

1. What holiday do you/does your friend celebrate?
2. Which religion celebrates this holiday?
3. What do you/does your friend do to celebrate this holiday?
4. Why do you/does your friend celebrate this holiday?

B. Make a list of holidays with your classmates.

_____

_____

_____

_____

Prompt 2

C. Read the prompt. Then complete the answers with your own information.

Talk about one of your country's national holidays.

What?	In my country, _____ is a national holiday.
When?	We celebrate _____.
Why?	We celebrate _____ because _____
	_____.
What?	Every year we _____.

Now practice your answers with a partner.

D. Make a list of things you do on holidays with a partner.

_____

_____

_____

_____

E. Read the prompt. Then underline the phrases you could use in your own answer.

Describe your favorite holiday. Include specific details and examples in your response.

Reasons you like holidays
- no school
- can eat a big dinner
- can see lots of family
- get presents
- makes me feel better
- enjoy the ceremony

Sample Response and Outline

F. Listen to the sample responses and complete the outlines. Track 28

Sample response 1		Sample response 2	
_____		_____	
What I do	**Why I like it**	**What I do**	**Why I like it**
_____	_____	_____	_____
_____	_____	_____	_____
_____	_____	_____	_____
_____	_____	_____	_____
_____	_____		

Conclusion: _____
_____

Conclusion: _____
_____

TOEFL Vocabulary Practice

G. Fill in the blanks with the correct words.

ceremonies	honor	resist	religion	national

1. Every country has different wedding _____.
2. Many people follow the rules of their _____ very strictly.
3. The BBC is the _____ TV channel for the United Kingdom.
4. Taking medicine helps the body _____ some diseases.
5. It is common to _____ great people by naming a street in a city after them.

Test

Step 1

Read the prompt.

> Describe your favorite holiday. Include specific details and examples in your response.

Step 2

Create an outline for your response.

_____

What I do

_____
_____
_____
_____

Why I like it

_____
_____
_____
_____

Conclusion: _____

_____

Step 3

Write a response using your outline from above.

My favorite holiday is _____.

Every year I _____

_____.

It's great because _____

_____.

But mostly, I love _____ because _____

_____.

Extension

Work with a partner. Take turns saying your response. Then change partners two more times. Time yourselves!

Your time: _____ seconds   Partner one's time: _____ seconds

Your time: _____ seconds   Partner two's time: _____ seconds

Your time: _____ seconds   Partner three's time: _____ seconds

Integrated

Getting Ready to Speak

A. Learn the words.

picnic	a meal had outdoors often in a park
hold	to host an event (past participle = held)
gymnasium	a building or room designed for playing sports
honestly	in an honest manner

voucher	a written certificate exchangeable for goods
attendance	the act of being at an event
essential	necessary
impose	to put on someone by authority
protest	to express objection

B. Read the announcement. Then answer the questions.

> **Beginning of Term Picnic**
>
> All students are invited to our "Beginning of Term Picnic." The picnic is on Friday at 12:30. It will be held at the east field outside the school gymnasium. We will have live entertainment and games with prizes. We will also be having a barbeque. You can choose from beef, chicken, and vegetarian burgers. Please pick up your meal voucher at the Student Union. We are sure that everyone in attendance will be satisfied!

1. What event is happening?

The _____..

2. What activities will be included?

There will be _____   _____.

3. What do you think the conversation will be about?

I think the conversation will be about _____.

Now practice the questions and answers with a partner.

C. Listen and repeat. Track 29

Practice

A. Read the announcement again and underline key information.

> ### Beginning of Term Picnic
>
> All students are invited to our "Beginning of Term Picnic." The picnic is on Friday at 12:30. It will be held at the east field outside the school gymnasium. We will have live entertainment and games with prizes. We will also be having a barbeque. You can choose from beef, chicken, and vegetarian burgers. Please pick up your meal voucher at the Student Union. We are sure that everyone in attendance will be satisfied!

Note-taking

B. Listen to the conversation and take notes. Track 30

Man	Woman
• Thinks the picnic is _____	• Knows there will be _____
• Thinks there are better ways to ____ _____	_____
• Thinks the university should buy___	• Thinks fun is _____
_____	• Thinks the man _____
• Knows the library needs _____	_____
_____	
• Thinks it's also _____	
_____	
• Thinks students should _____ not _____	
• Says his sister _____	
_____	
• Won't _____	
• Will write _____	

Prompt

C. Read the prompt.

> The man expresses his opinion of the announcement made about the beginning of term picnic. State his opinion and explain the reasons he gives for holding that opinion.

D. Listen to the sample response and complete the outline. `Track 31`

The man thinks the picnic is _____.

A. Thinks it is a waste

    1. of _money_____

    2. of _time_____ _____

B. The man says

    1. the university should buy _____

    2. the library needs _____

C. He decides that he won't _____

E. Now work with a partner. Take turns saying your own response using the outline from above.

Your time: _____ seconds   Your partner's time: _____ seconds

F. Fill in the blanks with the correct words.

attendance	essential	impose	protest	voucher

1. A meal _____ can be traded in for food in a cafeteria.

2. Many people _____ by carrying signs on the street.

3. Parents often _____ curfews on teenagers.

4. Perfect _____ is one way to ensure that you are learning the most you can in the classroom.

5. Having a passport is _____ when traveling.

Test

Step 1

Read the announcement.

> **Free On-campus Concert**
>
> A local rock band is holding a free concert. They will film the concert to use as a music video. The video will be shown on TV! The concert is next Wednesday at 4 p.m. and it will be held at the main gymnasium. The concert is free for students but it is essential you bring a voucher. Come to the campus events office on Wednesday morning to get your voucher. Bring your friends.

Step 2

Listen to the conversation and take notes. **Track 32**

Woman	Man
• Asks the man for a _____ _____	• Thinks the ticket will be _____ _____
• Wants to go at _____	• Has _____
• Wants to get _____ _____	_____
• Tells the man the concert is _____ _____	• Worries that he might _____ _____
• Invites the man to _____ _____	• Agrees to _____ _____
• Knows the concert is going to be __ _____	and to _____
• Convinces the man _____ _____	

Step 3

Read the prompt.

The woman expresses her opinion of the rock concert. State her opinion and explain the reasons she gives for holding that opinion.

Step 4

Create an outline for your response.

The woman is _____.

   A. The woman

      1. needs to go to _____

      2. wants to pick up _____

   B. She thinks the concert will be good because

      1. the tickets are _____

      2. the concert will be _____

Step 5

Write a response using your outline from above.

    The woman is _____.

She needs to go to _____

to _____.

She thinks the concert will be good because _____

and because _____.

Extension

Work with a partner. Take turns saying your response. Then change partners two more times. Time yourselves!

Your time: _____ seconds	Partner one's time: _____ seconds
Your time: _____ seconds	Partner two's time: _____ seconds
Your time: _____ seconds	Partner three's time: _____ seconds

Check-up

Fill in the blanks with the correct words.

gymnasium	held	honestly	picnic
holidays	celebration	pray	war

1. School sports are done in a _____.

2. Friendships are more successful when people speak _____ with one another.

3. Summer is a great time for a _____ at the beach.

4. Every four years, the Olympics are _____ in a different country.

5. Every year, millions of Muslims go to Mecca in Saudi Arabia to _____.

6. Germany and France have gone to _____ many times.

7. Many people do not have to work on national _____.

8. After winning the World Cup in 2006, Italy had a huge _____.

[06] Independent

Getting Ready to Speak

A. Learn the words.

Key Vocabulary

perhaps	maybe
opera	a style of singing
scenery	landscape or natural surroundings
surf	to ride the waves using a board

TOEFL Vocabulary

architecture	building design or style
fluent	to be able to speak a language with ease
immigrate	to move and settle in a new country
informal	unofficial; relaxed; casual
reside	to live somewhere

B. Read the prompt. Then answer the questions.

Talk about your city.

1. Which city do you live in?
   I live in _____.

2. What is your city famous for?
   My city is famous for _____.

3. Why should people visit your city?
   People should visit my city because _____
   _____.

Now practice the questions and answers with a partner.

C. Listen and repeat. Track 33

Practice

A. Read the prompt. Then take turns answering the questions with a partner.

> Talk about the most recent city that you have visited.

1. Where did you visit recently?
2. Why did you visit there?
3. What did you do while in that city?
4. Do you want to go back to that city? Why?

B. Make a list of characteristics that you look for in a city with your classmates.

_____

_____

_____

_____

Prompt 2

C. Read the prompt. Then complete the answers with your own information.

> Imagine you could build the best city in the world. What would it have?

How?   The buildings in my city would _____

_____.

Where?   I would build my city _____

_____.

What?   My city would have _____

_____.

Why?   My city would be special because _____

_____.

Now tell your answers to a partner.

D. Make a list of great things you have seen pictures of in other cities with a partner.

_____

_____

_____

_____

E. Read the prompt. Then underline the phrases you could use in your own response.

Describe the best city you have visited. Include specific details and examples in your response.

Reasons

- great atmosphere
- beautiful scenery
- great nightlife
- incredible food
- lots of live music
- very cheap

Sample Response and Outline

F. Listen to the sample responses and complete the outlines. `Track 34`

Sample response 1	Sample response 2

_____

_____

Reason 1   **Reason 2**   **Reason 1**   **Reason 2**

_____   _____   _____   _____
_____   _____   _____   _____
_____   _____   _____   _____

Support   **Support**   **Support**   **Support**

_____   _____   _____   _____
_____   _____   _____   _____

Conclusion: _____   **Conclusion:** _____

_____   _____

TOEFL Vocabulary Practice

G. Fill in the blanks with the correct words.

architecture   fluent   immigrate   informal   reside

1. ESL students rarely get opportunities to practice _____ English.
2. The Potato Famine from 1845 to 1851 caused many Irish to _____ to other countries.
3. The _____ of Paris's Louvre Museum mixed both old and new styles.
4. Most people who work in the United Nations are _____ in at least two languages.
5. Recently, many rich Russian businessmen have chosen to _____ in England rather than live in Russia.

Test

Step 1

Read the prompt.

> Describe the best city you have visited. Include specific details and examples in your response.

Step 2

Create an outline for your response.

_____

Reason 1

_____

Support _____

_____

Conclusion: _____

Reason 2

_____

Support _____

_____

_____

Step 3

Write a response using your outline from above.

The best city I have visited is _____.
It is amazing because _____
_____.
In addition, _____
_____
_____ is the best city.

Extension

Work with a partner. Take turns saying your response. Then change partners two more times. Time yourselves!

Your time: _____ seconds   Partner one's time: _____ seconds

Your time: _____ seconds   Partner two's time: _____ seconds

Your time: _____ seconds   Partner three's time: _____ seconds

Integrated

Getting Ready to Speak

A. Learn the words.

Key Vocabulary

molten	in a hot, thick, liquid state
seabed	the ground at the bottom of the sea
hotspot	a place where a particular activity frequently or easily takes place
dormant	temporarily inactive, as if sleeping

TOEFL Vocabulary

matter	a substance or material of a certain kind
explode	to blow up, burst, or shatter
climactic	extremely exciting or decisive
hazardous	very dangerous
repeatedly	again and again

B. Read the passage. Then answer the questions.

Volcanoes

Geology is the science of the solid matter that makes up the Earth. It looks at rocks and soils. The Earth is covered in a layer of rock like a crust. This is called the mantle. In some places, this crust is thin. This is where the molten rock under the surface, called magma, can escape. Once it reaches the surface, it explodes through the ground. This climactic event is called an eruption. The point where this happens is called a volcano.

1. What is geology the science of, and what does it look at?
   Geology is the science of the _____ that makes up the Earth. It looks at _____.

2. How does the molten rock escape when it reaches the Earth's surface?
   When molten rock reaches the Earth's surface, it _____.

3. What do you think the lecture will be about?
   I think that the lecture will be about _____.

Now practice the questions and answers with a partner.

C. Listen and repeat. `Track 35`

Practice

A. Read the passage again and underline the key information.

> ### Volcanoes
> Geology is the science of the solid matter that makes up the Earth. It looks at rocks and soils. The Earth is covered in a layer of rock like a crust. This is called the mantle. In some places, this crust is thin. This is where the molten rock under the surface, called magma, can escape. Once it reaches the surface, it explodes through the ground. This climactic event is called an eruption. The point where this happens is called a volcano.

Note-taking

B. Listen to the lecture and take notes. Track 36

Volcanoes

- An opening in the Earth's surface that _____
- The explosions can be _____
- They can be found _____

Mountains

- The explosions can cause _____
- This is because the molten rock _____

Causes

- Volcanoes can be caused by the movement of _____
- They can also occur where _____
- These places are called _____

Terms

- Volcanoes are called active when _____
- They are called dormant when _____
- The are called extinct when _____

Prompt

C. Read the prompt.

The professor and the passage give details about volcanoes. Explain how a volcanic eruption can cause mountains to form.

D. Listen to the sample response and complete the outline. `Track 37`

The lecture and the passage were about _____.

    A. Volcanoes

        1. occur when ____ _____

        _____

        2. are full of molten rock _____

        3. erupt with _____

    B. Volcanic eruptions

        1. can happen _____

        2. can cause _____

    C. Volcanoes appear

        1. when _____

        2. in places _____

    D. Volcanoes have different _____

    _____

E. Now work with a partner. Take turns saying your own response using the outline from above.

Your time: _____ seconds   Your partner's time: _____ seconds

F. Fill in the blanks with the correct words.

matter	explode	climactic	hazardous	repeatedly

1. In a movie, the most important part at the end is usually _____.

2. Many household chemicals can be _____ to our health if consumed.

3. When someone goes to the same store again and again, they go
_____.

4. When a firework or rocket is set on fire, it will _____.

5. _____ is the term used to describe any substance or material.

Test

Step 1

Read the passage.

Yellowstone Park

Supervolcanoes are the most hazardous volcanoes on Earth. When they explode they can change the whole world. The Yellowstone Caldera in the US is thought to be an active one. It has erupted three times in the last 2 million years. It is in the middle of a large park that is geologically active. It is well known all over the world. Old lava flows cover most of the land there. The energy from it heats thousands of springs and mud pools.

Step 2

Listen to the lecture and take notes. **Track 38**

Hotspots
- One of the best known is _____

Yellowstone Park
- It has several craters called _____
- The Yellowstone Caldera is _____

Supervolcanoes
- When they erupt _____
- They can _____

Yellowstone Caldera
- Has not erupted _____
- Under it is _____
- It is covered in _____

Geysers
- Are where hot water and _____
- There are _____

Step 3

Read the prompt.

The professor and the passage talk about Yellowstone Park. Explain what is there and how the park is geologically active.

Step 4

Create an outline for your response.

The lecture and the passage were about _____.

    A. Yellowstone Park

        1. Is said to be on _____

        2. Has several _____

    B. Yellowstone Caldera is _____

    C. Old lava covers _____

    D. Under the park _____

        1. This is covered _____

        2. It can escape _____

        3. This steam also heats _____

Step 5

Write a response using your outline from above.

>   The passage and the lecture were about _____.
> Underneath Yellowstone Park is one of the best known _____
> _____. The park has _____.
> One of them, called Yellowstone Caldera, is an _____.
> In the park, old lava _____.
> Underneath the park is _____,
> which is covered in _____. This can
> escape _____.
> The steam and magma also heat _____
> _____.

Extension

Work with a partner. Take turns saying your response. Then change partners two more times. Time yourselves!

Your time: _____ seconds   Partner one's time: _____ seconds

Your time: _____ seconds   Partner two's time: _____ seconds

Your time: _____ seconds   Partner three's time: _____ seconds

Check-up

Fill in the blanks with the correct words.

| molten | seabed | hotspot | dormant |
| surf | opera | scenery | perhaps |

1. When a ship on the sea sinks, it will do so until it finally hits the _____.

2. A very popular nightclub or restaurant could be called a social _____.

3. A volcano that has not erupted for a long time is called _____.

4. When metals like steel are made very hot, they turn to liquid. They become _____.

5. Pavarotti is one of the most famous names in _____.

6. Hawaii is one of the best places to _____ in the world.

7. Forest _____ in the fall is absolutely beautiful with all of the leaves changing colors.

8. _____ the air would be cleaner if we didn't have cars, but it would take a long time to get where we want to go.

Step 1

Read the prompt.

> Some people like happy endings in movies, others like sad endings. What do you prefer? Why?

Step 2

Create an outline for your response.

_____

Movies with happy endings   **Movies with sad endings**
Why:

_____   _____
_____   _____

Why not:

_____   _____
_____   _____

Better because: _____
_____

Step 3

Write a response using your outline from above.

> When I watch a movie, I prefer to _____.
> I like _____. I prefer not to watch
> _____ because they _____.
> I enjoy being able to watch a movie _____.

Work with a partner. Take turns saying your response. Then change partners two more times. Time yourselves!

Your time: _____ seconds   Partner one's time: _____ seconds
Your time: _____ seconds   Partner two's time: _____ seconds
Your time: _____ seconds   Partner three's time: _____ seconds

Step 1

Read the announcement.

> **Graduation Events**
>
> At the end of the term, the university will be hosting several events for the graduating class. One of the events is a ball. There is a limited amount of tickets so please buy them soon. Also, you must show proof you are graduating this term to be able to attend. If you are not graduating, then you cannot attend any of the events.

Step 2

Listen to the conversation and take notes. `Track 39`

Man	Woman
• Asks if attending _____ _____	• Not sure if attending. Depends on _____
• Asks why woman needs _____ _____ to go	• Should know by _____
• Going to school in summer is better than _____ _____	• Missing credits in _____ _____
• If not going to ball _____ _____	• The graduation ball is only for _____ _____

Step 3

Read the prompt.

The woman expresses that she is unable to attend the graduation ball. State the reason she will not be able to attend and how she feels about that.

Step 4

Create an outline for your response.

The conversation is about _____

_____.

    A. The woman might not _____

    B. She is waiting

        1. on _____

        2. to see whether _____

    C. The man thinks

        1. it is _____

        2. it would be _____

           rather than _____

Step 5

Write a response using your outline from above.

> The woman expresses that there is a chance she will not _____
> _____ because
> _____.
> She is waiting _____
> whether _____. She now needs to decide
> between _____.
> The man thinks it is _____ but thinks
> _____.

Extension

Work with a partner. Take turns saying your response. Then change partners two more times. Time yourselves!

Your time: _____ seconds   Partner one's time: _____ seconds

Your time: _____ seconds   Partner two's time: _____ seconds

Your time: _____ seconds   Partner three's time: _____ seconds

Step 1

Listen to the lecture and take notes. Track 40

- Botany is the study of plants
- There are _____ ways to _____
- Annuals, _____, and _____ are three categories that _____
- Trees and shrubs are usually _____
- Biennials produce leaves in first year and _____
  _____
- Annuals are less likely to _____

Step 2

Read the prompt.

> The professor explains the life span of plants and their ability to survive cold weather. Using points and examples from the lecture, describe why it is better for perennials to live in cold climates.

Step 3

Create an outline for your response.

The lecture is about botany and the life span of plants.

    A. Annuals

       1. live for _____

       2. are _____

    B. Perennials

       1. live _____

       2. are _____

    C. Biennials

       1. live _____

       2. are _____

Conclusion: Perennials and biennials are more likely to survive in the cold weather.

Step 4

Write a response using your outline.

> The lecture is about botany and the life span of plants. Plants can be categorized by their life span in three categories: _____
> _____.
> Annuals live _____. Perennials live _____
> _____, and biennials live _____.
> Annuals are the _____.
> Perennials and biennials are _____
> because they fall dormant in the wintertime.

Extension

Work with a partner. Take turns saying your response. Then change partners two more times. Time yourselves!

Your time: _____ seconds   Partner one's time: _____ seconds

Your time: _____ seconds   Partner two's time: _____ seconds

Your time: _____ seconds   Partner three's time: _____ seconds

Step 1

Read the prompt.

> Some people like being involved in school activities and others prefer their activities to be away from school. Describe your favorite activity. Who do you do it with and where do you do it?

Step 2

Create an outline for your response.

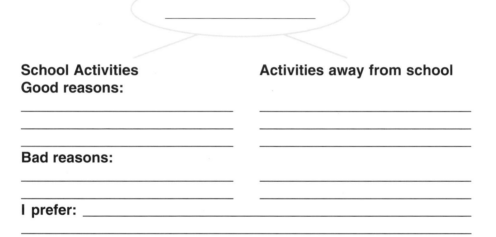

School Activities
Good reasons:

_____
_____

Bad reasons:

_____
_____

Activities away from school

_____
_____
_____

_____
_____

I prefer: _____
_____

Step 3

Write a response using your outline.

> I prefer to do _____.
> My favorite _____.
> _____. I get to _____
> I also like that I get to _____
> _____.

Work with a partner. Take turns saying your response. Then change partners two more times. Time yourselves!

Your time: _____ seconds	Partner one's time: _____ seconds
Your time: _____ seconds	Partner two's time: _____ seconds
Your time: _____ seconds	Partner three's time: _____ seconds

[07] Independent

Getting Ready to Speak

A. Learn the words.

Key Vocabulary

act	to do something
souvenir	something bought to remember a place
lonely	feeling alone or isolated
homesick	longing to be at home

TOEFL Vocabulary

tour	a trip visiting several places
guide	a person who leads tourists
impulse	a sudden urge
appropriate	fitting or suitable
investigate	to take a look; to examine

B. Read the prompt. Then answer the questions.

Talk about the last place that you traveled to.

1. Where did you last travel to?
   I last traveled to _____.

2. Who did you go with?
   I went with _____.

3. How could your vacation have been better?
   My vacation could have been better if ___ _____.

Now practice the questions and answers with a partner.

C. Listen and repeat. Track 41

Practice

Prompt 1

A. Read the prompt. Then take turns answering the questions with a partner.

Talk about traveling alone and traveling in a group.

1. What is the best thing about traveling alone?
2. What is the worst thing about traveling alone?
3. What is the best thing about traveling with a tour?
4. What is the worst thing about traveling with a tour?

B. Make a list with your classmates of problems that can occur when traveling.

_____

_____

_____

_____

Prompt 2

C. Read the prompt. Then complete the answers with your own information.

Talk about where you would go on your perfect vacation.

Where?   I would go to _____.

Who?   I would go with _____.

Why?   I would go with _____ because _____.

What?   I would want to see _____.

Now practice your answers with a partner.

D. Make a list with a partner of things that you like to do when traveling.

_____

_____

_____

_____

E. Read the prompt. Then underline the phrases you could use in your own response.

Is it better to travel alone or with a tour group? Give specific examples.

Reasons to travel alone or with a tour group

- go where I want to go
- can sleep in
- can decide my own route
- can be alone if I want
- don't have to worry about things
- can always join late

Sample Response and Outline

F. Listen to the sample responses and complete the outlines. Track 42

Sample response 1

_____

Reason 1	Reason 2
_____	_____
_____	_____
Support _____	Support _____
_____	_____
_____	_____

Conclusion: _____

Sample response 2

_____

Reason 1	Reason 2
_____	_____
_____	_____
Support _____	Support _____
_____	_____
_____	_____

Conclusion: _____

TOEFL Vocabulary Practice

G. Fill in the blanks with the correct words.

guide   impulses   appropriate   investigate   tours

1. Detectives always _____ an area when something bad happens.

2. A _____ can usually tell you lots of good information that many books do not tell you.

3. Sometimes _____ can be a cheaper way to travel than going by yourself.

4. Children often find it difficult to control their _____.

5. When you go to work, you should wear clothes that are _____ for the job.

Test

Step 1

Read the prompt.

Is it better to travel alone or with a tour group? Give specific examples.

Step 2

Create an outline for your response.

_____

Reason 1

_____

_____

Support _____

_____

_____

Reason 2

_____

_____

Support _____

_____

_____

Conclusion: _____

_____

Step 3

Write a response using your outline from above.

When traveling, I think it's better to _____

_____.

Going _____

_____.

Once you decide _____

_____.

The best way to travel is _____.

Extension

Work with a partner. Take turns saying your response. Then change partners two more times. Time yourselves!

Your time: _____ seconds   Partner one's time: _____ seconds

Your time: _____ seconds   Partner two's time: _____ seconds

Your time: _____ seconds   Partner three's time: _____ seconds

Integrated

Getting Ready to Speak

A. Learn the words.

frustrated	feeling discouraged or disappointed
quarter	one fourth of something
syllabus	an outline for a course
quit	to stop or give something up

anthropology	the study of human beings
passion	a powerful feeling or desire
qualify	to show necessary ability in a preliminary contest
coach	a person who teaches a sport
absence	failure to attend

B. Listen to the first part of a conversation. Then answer the questions. `Track 43`

1. What are the students discussing?
   The students are discussing _____.

2. What does the woman have at the same time?
   The woman has _____.

3. What do you think the rest of the conversation will be about?
   I think the rest of the conversation will be about _____
   _____.

4. Which do you think the woman should choose?
   I think the woman should choose _____.

Now practice the questions and answers with a partner.

C. Listen and repeat. `Track 44`

Practice

A. Listen to the full conversation and take notes. `Track 45`

Reasons for taking the class	Reasons for going to practice
• Professor is _____ _____	• Basketball is _____ _____
• Would learn _____	• Been playing _____ _____
• Student needs _____	• Wants to _____ _____
• Loved _____ _____	• Came to school _____ _____

B. Use your notes to complete the answers.

1. What are some of the reasons the students discuss for taking the class?

   The students discuss _____

   _____.

2. What are some of the reasons the student should attend basketball practice?

   The student should go to practice because _____

   _____.

Now practice the questions and answers with a partner.

C. Read the prompt.

> The students discuss whether the woman should take an anthropology course or go to basketball practice. Describe the reasons for each choice. Then state which you think is the better option.

D. Listen to the sample response and complete the outline. `Track 46`

The conversation is about _____.

    A. Should take the course because

        1. the teacher is _____

        2. the student needs _____ _____

        3. she really _____

    B. Should go to basketball practice because

        1. it is her _____

        2. she has been _____

        3. she has to _____

        4. she has a _____

Conclusion: I think _____

        because _____.

E. Write your own conclusion using the outline from above.

Conclusion: I think _____

because _____.

F. Now work with a partner. Take turns saying your own response using the outline from above.

Your time: _____ seconds   Your partner's time: _____ seconds

G. Fill in the blanks with the correct words.

absence   anthropology   coach   passion   qualify

1. Every sports team needs a _____.

2. In a small class, teachers notice every _____.

3. It is important to have a _____ for what you do.

4. It is very difficult to _____ for the Olympic Games.

5. _____ is the study of humans.

Test

Step 1

Woman	Man
• Wants the man to _____ _____	• Has _____
	• Is the _____
• Her birthday is _____ _____	of his _____
	• Tomorrow is _____
• Thinks there must be _____ _____	_____
	• Knows his brother will _____
• Other friends will _____ _____	_____
	• Should keep _____
	_____

Step 2

Read the prompt.

> The students are discussing the man's plans for tomorrow. Discuss each student's opinion. Then state what you think the man should do and why.

Step 3

Create an outline for your response.

The conversation is about _____.

    A. The woman

        1. wants the man to _____ because _____

        2. thinks there must be _____

        3. knows their friends will _____

    B. The man

        1. is the _____

        2. knows tomorrow is _____

        3. knows his brother _____

        4. wants to _____

Conclusion: I think _____
_____.

Step 4

Write a response using your outline.

The conversation is about _____.
The woman wants the man to _____
because _____ _____. She thinks that
there _____, so _____ _____.
Also, their friends will be _____.
The man has to _____ because tomorrow _____
_____. His brother _____
if _____ and he wants to _____.
I think the man should _____
because _____.

Extension

Work with a partner. Take turns saying your answer. Then change partners two more times. Time yourselves!

Your time: _____ seconds   Partner one's time: _____ seconds
Your time: _____ seconds   Partner two's time: _____ seconds
Your time: _____ seconds   Partner three's time: _____ seconds

Check-up

Fill in the blanks with the correct words.

lonely	frustrated	souvenirs	quarter
act	quit	syllabus	homesick

1. When something becomes difficult, you shouldn't _____.
2. If you live in a foreign country for a long time, you may become _____.
3. It's important to read the _____ carefully when you start a new class.
4. When things don't work properly, people can become _____ quickly.
5. People who move to a new city without any friends can often feel _____.
6. Many people bring back _____ for their friends from their vacations.
7. Three months is a _____ of a year.
8. Puppies often _____ badly. They must learn how to be good.

[08] Independent

Getting Ready to Speak

A. Learn the words.

Key Vocabulary

keen	eager or enthusiastic
distract	to take someone's attention away from what he or she is doing
preparation	the work and planning needed before starting something
unclear	not understandable; confusing

TOEFL Vocabulary

extend	to make longer
anticipate	to expect or look forward to something
inevitably	happening without chance of avoiding it
curriculum	the subjects or topics taught in a class
regret	to feel sorry for a past act

B. Read the prompt. Then answer the questions.

Talk about what you do before you take a test.

1. When do you normally start studying for a test?
   I normally start studying for a test _____.

2. What do you do to prepare for the test?
   I prepare for my test by _____.

3. How do you normally feel before taking a test?
   I normally feel _____ before taking a test.

Now practice the questions and answers with a partner.

C. Listen and repeat. Track 48

Practice

👤👤 **A. Read the prompt. Then take turns answering the questions with a partner.**

> What are some good and bad things about studying at home and at school for tests?

1. What is a good thing about studying at home for a test?

2. What is a bad thing about studying at home for a test?

3. What is a good thing about studying at school for a test?

4. What is a bad thing about studying at school for a test?

B. Make a list of things to do to study for a test with your classmates.

_____

_____

_____

_____

Prompt 2

C. Read the prompt. Then complete the answers with your own information.

> Talk about the last test that you studied for.

What?	I studied for my _____ test.
Where?	For my _____ test, I studied at _____.
How long?	I studied for _____.
How?	I did _____ on my test.

👤👤 **Now practice your answers with a partner.**

D. Make a list of emotions that you feel before, during, and after a test with a partner.

_____

_____

_____

_____

E. Read the prompt. Then underline the phrases you could use in your own response.

Some students like to prepare for tests at home. Others prefer to study for tests at school. Which method of test preparation do you think is better? Why?

Reasons to prepare at home or at school

- friends can distract me
- easier preparation
- easy to find things that are needed
- always get help
- stay up late to study
- don't have to waste time going to a new place

Sample Response and Outline

F. Listen to the sample responses and complete the outlines. Track 49

Sample response 1	Sample response 2
_____	_____

Reason 1	Reason 2	Reason 1	Reason 2
_____	_____	_____	_____
_____	_____	_____	_____
Support _____	Support _____	Support _____	Support _____
_____	_____	_____	_____
_____	_____	_____	_____

Conclusion: _____

Conclusion: _____

TOEFL Vocabulary Practice

G. Fill in the blanks with the correct words.

extend	anticipate	curriculum	regret	inevitably

1. Telephone companies did not _____ how popular text messaging would become.
2. Older people sometimes _____ that they did not do things differently when they were younger.
3. Every university has its own unique _____.
4. Eating healthier foods _____ leads to stronger, healthier people.
5. People in jail rarely want to _____ their time.

Test

Step 1

Read the prompt.

> Some students like to prepare for tests at home. Others prefer to study for tests at school. Which method of test preparation do you think is better? Why?

Step 2

Create an outline for your response.

_____

Reason 1

_____

_____

Support _____

_____

_____

Reason 2

_____

_____

Support _____

_____

_____

Conclusion: _____

_____

Step 3

Write a response using your outline from above.

The best place for me to study is _____.
I am always keen to study at _____ because _____
_____.
More importantly, _____
_____.
Studying at the _____ is the best.

Work with a partner. Take turns saying your response. Then change partners two more times. Time yourselves!

Your time: _____ seconds

Your time: _____ seconds

Your time: _____ seconds

Partner one's time: _____ seconds

Partner two's time: _____ seconds

Partner three's time: _____ seconds

Getting Ready to Speak

A. Learn the words.

Key Vocabulary

brilliant	exceptionally smart
detective	someone who investigates when something wrong happens
clue	something that helps to understand or solve a mystery
partner	someone who shares an activity with another person

TOEFL Vocabulary

analyze	to study something closely
vague	not clear in meaning
predict	to say what will happen; to guess
implicate	to show how something or someone is connected to something or someone else
scheme	a secret plan, usually to commit some crime

B. Listen to the first part of a lecture. Then answer the questions. Track 50

1. What is the lecture mainly about?
The lecture is mainly about _____.

2. What did Bronte, Wordsworth, and Wells all do?
The authors all _____.

3. What else do you think the professor will discuss in this lecture?
I think the professor will discuss _____.

Now practice the questions and answers with a partner.

C. Listen and repeat. Track 51

Practice

A. Listen to the full lecture and take notes. `Track 52`

- Sherlock Holmes was created _____
- Holmes was a _____

  _____

- He was able to _____
- The last explanation _____
- His friend, _____
- His enemy, _____
- Holmes often _____
- People still _____

B. Use your notes to complete the answers.

1. How was Holmes able to predict what happened?

   He was able to predict what happened because _____.

2. What does Sherlock Holmes look like?

   Sherlock Holmes often wore _____.

Now practice the questions and answers with a partner.

C. Read the prompt.

> The professor talked about Sherlock Holmes in the lecture. Using examples from the lecture, talk about why Sherlock Holmes is so famous.

D. Listen to the sample response and complete the outline. `Track 53`

The lecture is about _____.

A. Analyzing clues

    1. Holmes analyzed clues _____

    2. He was usually _____

    3. The last explanation usually _____

B. About Holmes

    1. Friend: _____

    2. Enemy: _____

    3. Clothes and Habits: _____

Conclusion: People still _____

_____.

E. Now work with a partner. Take turns saying your own response using the outline from above.

Your time: _____ seconds   Your partner's time: _____ seconds

F. Fill in the blanks with the correct words.

analyze	vague	predict	implicated	schemes

1. Fortune-tellers say that they can _____ the future.

2. The mafia is involved in many _____ to make money.

3. School teaches children to _____ a problem and then figure out how to solve that problem.

4. Many people think that politicians give _____ answers to difficult questions.

5. The criminal was _____ in a crime.

Test

Step 1

Listen to the lecture and take notes. **Track 54**

- Arthur Conan Doyle led a very interesting life.
- He was born in _____
- He went to university _____
- He wrote _____
- It was called _____
- He used his fame _____
- He helped people who _____
- He ran for _____
- Idea of Holmes is _____
- May have come from one of his _____
- May have come from Edgar Allen Poe's _____
- Holmes and Doyle were equally brilliant men.

Step 2

Read the prompt.

> The professor describes Arthur Conan Doyle's life. Using examples from the lecture, describe how Doyle's life was interesting.

Step 3

Create an outline for your response.

The lecture is about Arthur Conan Doyle's interesting life.

    A. His life

        1. Was born in _____

        2. Went to university to be a _____

        3. Wrote first story in _____

             • It was called _____

             • It was very _____

        4. He helped others

             • He helped people who were _____

             • He helped them to be _____

        5. He ran for _____

    B. His idea for Holmes is _____

        1. One of his _____

        2. Edgar Allen _____

Conclusion: Holmes was a brilliant man. Doyle was an equally brilliant man.

Step 4

Write a response using your outline.

The lecture is about _____.
He was _____. He went to university _____.
He wrote his first story _____. It was very popular and was called
_____. He became very famous.
He used this _____. He helped people _____
_____. He helped them to be free. Later he tried to run
_____. His idea for Holmes is _____
_____. People say he is based _____.
Doyle loved to read _____,
so his idea for Holmes may have come from him. Holmes was a brilliant detective.
Doyle was also a brilliant man.

Extension

Work with a partner. Take turns saying your response. Then change partners two more times. Time yourselves!

Your time: _____ seconds   Partner one's time: _____ seconds
Your time: _____ seconds   Partner two's time: _____ seconds
Your time: _____ seconds   Partner three's time: _____ seconds

Check-up

Fill in the blanks with the correct words.

brilliant	detective	partner	clues
distract	preparation	unclear	keen

1. After a crime occurs, a _____ usually comes to find out what happened.

2. It is much easier to row a canoe with a _____ than doing it by yourself.

3. Leonardo Da Vinci was a _____ artist, sculptor, and scientist.

4. Fingerprints are one of the first _____ that police look for at a crime scene.

5. Children are often _____ to play games.

6. Loud students often _____ other students who are trying to study.

7. Often people read about where they are going in _____ for going on vacation.

8. Even now, doctors are still _____ about exactly how the brain works.

[09] Independent

Getting Ready to Speak

A. Learn the words.

Key Vocabulary

favorable	approving; advantageous
surround	to be in the space around someone or something
location	the position or place where something is
absolutely	emphatically true; without doubt

TOEFL Vocabulary

prominent	well-known; distinguished
hesitate	to delay briefly because of fear or doubt
focal point	the center of attention
equip	to provide with things that are needed
likewise	in the same way; also

B. Read the prompt. Then answer the questions.

Talk about the most prominent university in your country.

1. Which university is it?
   The most prominent university in my country is _____.

2. What kind of city is this university located in?
   It is located in a _____.

3. Do you want to go to this university? Why or why not?
   I do/don't want to go to this university because _____.

👤👤 **Now practice the questions and answers with a partner.**

🎧 **C. Listen and repeat.** Track 55

Practice

Prompt 1

A. **Read the prompt. Take turns answering the questions with a partner.**

Talk about some good and bad things about living in both a big and small city.

1. What is a good thing about living in a big city?
2. What is a bad thing about living in a big city?
3. What is a good thing about living in a small city?
4. What is a bad thing about living in a small city?

B. **Make a list of fun things you can do in a big city and a small city with your classmates.**

_____

_____

_____

_____

Prompt 2

C. **Read the prompt. Then complete the answers with your own information.**

Talk about the university that you want to go to.

Which?   I want to go to _____.

Where?   It is located in _____.

What?   I want to study _____.

Why?   I want to go to _____ because _____.

Now practice your answers with a partner.

D. **Make a list of things that you want to do while in university with a partner.**

_____

_____

_____

_____

E. Read the prompt. Then underline the phrases you could use in your own response.

> Do you want to go to university in a big or small city? Why?

Reasons for going to university in a big or small city

- favorable study environment
- opportunities after finishing university
- great location
- internships
- sense of community
- can feel lost

Sample Response and Outline

F. Now listen to the sample responses and complete the outlines. [Track 56]

Sample response 1

⬭ _____

Reason 1
_____
_____
_____

Reason 2
_____
_____
_____

Support _____
_____
_____

Support _____
_____
_____

Conclusion: _____
_____

Sample response 2

⬭ _____

Reason 1
_____
_____
_____

Reason 2
_____
_____
_____

Support _____
_____
_____

Support _____
_____
_____

Conclusion: _____
_____

TOEFL Vocabulary Practice

G. Fill in the blanks with the correct words.

hesitate   equipped   prominent   focal point   likewise

1. During the 1960s Pele was the _____ of the Brazilian soccer team's offense.

2. Rich countries are much better _____ to deal with disasters than poor ones are.

3. Many _____ scientists like Einstein, Bohr, and Fermi have won the Nobel Prize.

4. Many parents _____ to let their children drive a car for the first time.

5. In the fifteenth and sixteenth centuries, Spain sent sailors around the world to claim new land. _____, Portugal also took a lot of land.

Test

Step 1

Read the prompt.

> Do you want to go to university in a big or small city? Why?

Step 2

Create an outline for your response.

_____

Reason 1

_____

_____

Support _____

_____

Conclusion: _____

_____

Reason 2

_____

_____

Support _____

_____

Step 3

Write a response using your outline from above.

I want to go to university in _____ city.
_____ cities are best equipped for me because _____
_____.
Likewise, _____
_____.
So, _____ cities are best for me.

Extension

Work with a partner. Take turns saying your response. Then change partners two more times. Time yourselves!

Your time: _____ seconds	Partner one's time: _____ seconds
Your time: _____ seconds	Partner two's time: _____ seconds
Your time: _____ seconds	Partner three's time: _____ seconds

Integrated

Getting Ready to Speak

A. Learn the words.

Key Vocabulary

renovate	to change or improve a building/room
opposition	an opposite idea or feeling; resistance
advisor	a person who gives help or advice
beneficial	advantageous; helpful

TOEFL Vocabulary

interact	to communicate or act with others
resident	a person living in a certain place
justification	a reason for doing something
occupy	to be in a space
hence	for this reason; therefore

B. Read the announcement. Then answer the questions.

> ### Dormitory Games Room
> There will be a new games room created in our dorm. It will open in September. An old living space will be renovated. This room will have a pool table, card tables, and other activities. Students will be able to interact with one another here. We hope this will help build a strong community. Please send any opposition to this plan to the resident advisor.

1. What will happen?
   A new games room will _____.

2. What activities will take place in the games room?
   Students can play _____.

3. What do you think the conversation will be about?
   I think the conversation will be about _____.

Now practice the questions and answers with a partner.

C. Listen and repeat. Track 57

Practice

A. Read the announcement again and underline the key information.

> **Dormitory Games Room**
>
> There will be a new games room created in our dorm. It will open in September. An old living space will be renovated. This room will have a pool table, card tables, and other activities. Students will be able to interact with one another here. We hope this will help build a strong community. Please send any opposition to this plan to the resident advisor.

Note-taking

B. Listen to the conversation and take notes. Track 58

Man	Woman
• Thinks the games room will _____ _____	• Doesn't _____
• Can't wait for _____ _____	• Thinks students should _____ _____ not _____
• Thinks both _____ and _____ are important	• Thinks it sounds like _____ _____
• Needs _____	
• Usually goes _____ _____	
• This is better because _____ _____	
• Can spend free time _____ _____	
• Might make _____	

Prompt

C. Read the prompt.

> The man expresses his opinion of the announcement made about the new dormitory games room. State his opinion and explain the reasons he gives for holding that opinion.

D. Listen to the sample response and complete the outline. `Track 59`

Opinion: The man thinks the new games room is _____.

   Λ. It is better because he

      1. won't _____ _____

      2. can take a break and _____ _____

   B. The man might

      1. meet _____

      2. meet _____

   C. He thinks the new games room will be _____

Speaking Practice

E. Now work with a partner. Take turns saying your own response using the outline from above.

Your time: _____ seconds   Your partner's time: _____ seconds

TOEFL Vocabulary Practice

F. Fill in the blanks with the correct words.

     hence   interact   justification   occupied   residents

1. When learning a new language you should _____ with native speakers.

2. Radiation is dangerous. _____, we protect ourselves from it.

3. Students living in a dormitory are _____ of the university.

4. It is annoying when all parking spaces are _____.

5. A heart attack can be a _____ for an operation.

Test

Step 1

Read the announcement.

> ### Additions to the Dorm Lounge
>
> The dorm council has decided to renovate the dorm lounge. The focus of this project will be a new entertainment unit. The unit will hold a new television and DVD player. They will be added next month. Now students will have a place to study and relax. Hence, this will be good for all students occupying the lounge. Dorm residents can use the new equipment anytime.

Step 2

Listen to the conversation and take notes. `Track 60`

Woman	Man
• Learns that dorm council is _____ _____ and _____ • Thinks it's _____ • Thinks the lounge is for _____ _____ • Knows that people can't _____ _____ • Usually _____ _____ • Thinks it's a _____	• Thinks it will be _____ _____ • Believes that more people will _____ _____ • Wants to know _____ _____ • Thinks the woman should _____ _____ _____

Step 3

Read the prompt.

The woman expresses her opinion of the announcement made about the additions to the dorm lounge. State her opinion and explain the reasons she gives for holding that opinion.

Step 4

Create an outline for your response.

Opinion: The woman is _____.

    A. The woman thinks the dorm lounge

        1. is for _____

        2. is not for _____

    B. She goes there

        1. to _____

        2. to _____

Step 5

Write a response using your outline from above.

> The woman is _____
> _____.
> She goes there to _____ not to _____.
> She thinks people can't _____.
> She goes to the lounge to _____.
> She will probably _____
> _____.

👤👤 **Work with a partner. Take turns saying your response. Then change partners two more times. Time yourselves!**

Your time: _____ seconds   Partner one's time: _____ seconds

Your time: _____ seconds   Partner two's time: _____ seconds

Your time: _____ seconds   Partner three's time: _____ seconds

Check-up

Fill in the blanks with the correct words.

advisor	beneficial	opposition	renovate
location	absolutely	surrounds	favorable

1. Many people _____ after buying a house.
2. Learning English can be very _____.
3. If you don't know what courses to take, you should speak to an _____.
4. There is a lot of _____ to an idea in a debate.
5. A _____ review in a newspaper can often help a new restaurant do well.
6. With fruit, we usually eat the part that _____ the seed.
7. Pirate maps usually show the _____ of a great treasure.
8. Wayne Gretzky is considered to be _____ the best hockey player of all time.

[10] Independent

Getting Ready to Speak

A. Learn the words.

Key Vocabulary

direct	without interfering people, factors, or influences
proud	feeling pleased, satisfied, and happy
enrich	to make better
sculpture	a three-dimensional piece of art

TOEFL Vocabulary

whereas	in contrast; on the other hand
societal	for society
grand	impressive; wonderful
temporary	not lasting for a long time
tourism	the industry of people traveling for pleasure

B. Read the prompt. Then answer the questions.

Talk about your art experiences.

1. What is your favorite kind of art to look at? Why?
   My favorite art to look at _____ because _____.

2. What is your favorite kind of art to make? Why?
   My favorite art to make _____ because _____.

3. Where is the closest art museum to where you live?
   The closest art museum to my home is _____.

Now practice the questions and answers with a partner.

C. Listen and repeat. Track 61

Practice

A. Read the prompt. Then take turns answering the questions with a partner.

Talk about the last art museum that you went to.

1. What was the last art museum that you went to?
2. When did you go there?
3. What was your favorite thing/ things that you saw in the museum?
4. Do you want to go back to the museum? Why?

B. Make a list of emotions that you feel when you are at the museum with your classmates.

_____

_____

_____

_____

Prompt 2

C. Read the prompt. Then complete the answers with your own information.

Talk about what you want to see improved in your city.

What?   I want to improve _____ in my city.

When?   This should happen _____.

How?   My city can do this by _____.

Why?   I want to _____ because _____.

Now practice your answers with a partner.

D. Make a list of problems that you see in your city with a partner.

_____

_____

_____

_____

E. Read the prompt. Then underline the phrases you could use in your own response.

Should cities invest in art and art museums or spend their money on other things? Why?

Reasons to spend or not spend money

- increases education
- creates societal pride
- makes cities prettier
- is less important
- makes cities more interesting
- doesn't make many jobs

Sample Response and Outline

F. Now listen to the sample responses and complete the outlines. Track 62

Sample response 1	Sample response 2

_____

Reason 1
_____
_____

Reason 2
_____
_____

Support _____
_____

Support _____
_____

Conclusion: _____
_____

Reason 1
_____
_____

Reason 2
_____
_____

Support _____
_____

Support _____
_____

Conclusion: _____
_____

TOEFL Vocabulary Practice

G. Fill in the blanks with the correct words.

whereas   societal   grand   temporary   tourism

1. The government needs to take care of _____ needs.
2. Not eating for a day or two is only a _____ way to lose weight.
3. Greece makes more money from _____ than anything else.
4. American Thanksgiving is celebrated in November. _____ Korean Thanksgiving is usually celebrated in September.
5. A _____ buffet usually has too much food to choose from.

Test

Step 1

Read the prompt.

> Should cities invest in art and art museums or spend their money on other things? Why?

Step 2

Create an outline for your response.

◯ _____

Reason 1

_____

_____

Support _____

_____

_____

Reason 2

_____

_____

Support _____

_____

_____

Conclusion: _____

_____

Step 3

Write a response using your outline from above.

Cities should spend their money on _____.

This is because _____

_____.

In addition, _____

_____.

Public money should be used on _____

_____.

Extension

Work with a partner. Take turns saying your response. Then change partners two more times. Time yourselves!

Your time: _____ seconds   Partner one's time: _____ seconds

Your time: _____ seconds   Partner two's time: _____ seconds

Your time: _____ seconds   Partner three's time: _____ seconds

Integrated

Getting Ready to Speak

A. Learn the words.

combat	a fight between two groups, especially between soldiers
Coast Guard	an emergency service that rescues people in difficulties at sea
independence	the condition of being free from control by another person, organization, or state
allied	joined in alliance with other nations, people, or groups

armed forces	the combined bodies of land, sea, and air troops of a country
voluntary	acting by choice rather than by external pressure
defense	the protection of something, especially from attack by another
civil	relating to what happens within a state or between different groups of citizens
overseas	across or beyond a sea, especially in another country

B. Read the passage. Then answer the questions.

US Armed Forces

The US military is the second largest in the world. It has around 1.5 million members. It is a voluntary military. This means that it is up to each person if he or she wants to join. It was first formed in 1775 to fight in the conflict against Great Britain. The US armed forces are made up of five branches. They include the army, navy, and air force. Every part is run by the US president. Most branches are part of the US Department of Defense.

1. When was the US military first formed?
   The US military was first formed in _____.
2. Who runs the US armed forces?
   The US armed forces are run by _____ _____.
3. What do you think the lecture will be about?
   I think that the lecture will be about _____.

Now practice the questions and answers with a partner.

C. Listen and repeat. Track 63

Practice

A. Read the passage again and underline the key information.

> ### US Armed Forces
>
> The US military is the second largest in the world. It has around 1.5 million members. It is a voluntary military. This means that it is up to each person if he or she wants to join. It was first formed in 1775 to fight in the conflict against Great Britain. The US armed forces are made up of five branches. They include the army, navy, and air force. Every part is run by the US president. Most branches are part of the US Department of Defense.

Note-taking

B. Listen to the lecture and take notes. Track 64

The US armed forces

- Are seen as _____
- To join them is _____

The US

- Spends more money _____
- Armed forces are made up of _____

    _____

History of the US military

- Was formed to _____
- Later took part in _____
- Grew larger in the _____
- Played a big part in the _____

The US president

- Is the _____
- The heads of the different parts _____

Prompt

C. Read the prompt.

> The professor and the passage give details about the US armed forces. Explain how the US armed forces formed and grew to become the most powerful military in the world.

D. Listen to the sample response and complete the outline. `Track 65`

The lecture and the passage were about _____.

    A. The US armed forces

        1. Formed in _____

        2. Were formed to _____

        3. Later fought in the _____

    B. The early twentieth century

        1. Forces grew _____

        2. Helped the _____

    C. US armed forces today

        1. Has around _____

        2. The US spends _____

The US armed forces are run by _____.

E. Now work with a partner. Take turns saying your own response using the outline from above.

Your time: _____ seconds   Your partner's time: _____ seconds

F. Fill in the blanks with the correct words.

armed forces   voluntary   defense   civil   overseas

1. Some people like to do _____ work, like serving food to homeless people.

2. In the military, soldiers often have to leave their families to serve _____.

3. _____ war can occur when the citizens of a country fight over what they believe is right.

4. In some countries, citizens must serve in the _____ for a certain amount of time.

5. Hundreds of years ago, castles were built with very high walls as a form of _____ from enemies.

Test

Step 1

Read the passage.

> ### US Coast Guard
>
> The US Coast Guard is a branch of the US armed forces. It was first formed around the end of the War of Independence in 1790. It has many different missions. One of the main ones is that of search and rescue. Others include defense readiness and work as a law agency. It is the smallest of all the armed forces. Their motto is "Always Ready." In times of war, it is controlled by the US Navy.

Step 2

Listen to the lecture and take notes. **Track 66**

The US Coast Guard
- Was formed _____
- Its ships _____

The modern US Coast Guard
- Set up as _____
- Main jobs are _____
  _____
- Can do this _____
- It is both _____

The Coast Guard in Conflict
- Has been involved in _____
- Helped to land _____

The Coast Guard Today
- One of its main jobs _____
- It has _____
- Answers to _____

Step 3

Read the prompt.

> The professor and the passage talk about the US Coast Guard. Explain its role and history in the US armed forces.

Step 4

Create an outline for your response.

The passage and lecture were about _____.

    A. It was formed _____

    B. The modern Coast Guard

        1. Was set up as _____

        2. Its main missions _____

            _____

        3. Is both _____

    C. Is the smallest _____

    D. One of its main jobs _____

        _____

    E. Is controlled by the _____

    F. During wars its control _____

Step 5

Write a response using your outline from above.

>   The passage and lecture were about _____.
> It was first formed in _____. Later, the modern Coast Guard was
> set up as _____.
> Then its main missions were to _____.
> Today, it is both a _____ and _____.
> It is the smallest of all _____ and one of its main
> jobs is _____.
> It is controlled by the _____.
> In times of war it is _____.

Extension

👤👤 **Work with a partner. Take turns saying your response. Then change partners two more times. Time yourselves!**

Your time: _____ seconds	Partner one's time: _____ seconds
Your time: _____ seconds	Partner two's time: _____ seconds
Your time: _____ seconds	Partner three's time: _____ seconds

Check-up

Fill in the blanks with the correct words.

combat	Coast Guard	independence	allied
proud	enriched	direct	sculptures

1. The winning side in World War II were the _____ forces.

2. When two groups fight against each other, they go into _____.

3. When a state or area in a country becomes its own country, it gains _____.

4. Search and rescue at sea is one of the main jobs of the _____.

5. Milk is often _____ with other things to make it even stronger.

6. Most people feel incredibly _____ after graduating from university.

7. Michelangelo's *David* is one of the most famous _____ in the world.

8. Doing homework usually has a _____ effect on a person's grade in a class.

[11] Independent

Getting Ready to Speak

A. Learn the words.

Key Vocabulary

member	a person in a group
rarely	almost never
extremely	very
continue	to keep going

TOEFL Vocabulary

controversy	a widespread disagreement on a difficult topic
enthusiastic	showing excitement or interest
instruct	to tell someone to do something
incentive	something that encourages someone to do something
dismiss	to refuse to consider something

B. Read the prompt. Then answer the questions.

Talk about a group that you are a part of.

1. What is the name of your group?
   The name of my group is _____.
2. What do you do?
   We _____.
3. Why do you continue to be a part of the group?
   I continue to be a part of the group because _____.

Now practice the questions and answers with a partner.

C. **Listen and repeat.** Track 67

Practice

Prompt 1

A. Read the prompt. Then take turns answering the questions with a partner.

> Talk about how you normally act when you are with a group of friends.

1. How often do you suggest ideas?
2. How do you feel when the group does something you don't really want to do?
3. Are you happier being the leader of the group or a regular member?
4. When do you feel it is important that the group does what you want?

B. Make a list of things that are better done in a group with your classmates.

_____

_____

_____

_____

Prompt 2

C. Read the prompt. Then complete the answers with your own information.

> Talk about your experiences as a leader.

When?	I was a leader _____.
How?	I became the leader by _____.
What ?	As a leader I _____.
Why?	I liked/didn't like being the leader because _____.

Now practice your answers with a partner.

D. Make a list of responsibilities that the leader of a group has with a partner.

_____

_____

_____

_____

E. Read the prompt. Then underline the phrases you could use in your own response.

Is it better to be the leader of a group or a member of a group? Why?

Reasons to be a leader or a member
- more responsibility
- too much attention
- receive a lot of praise
- dismiss my ideas
- too much stress
- a lot of extra work

Sample Response and Outline

F. Now listen to the sample responses and complete the outlines. Track 68

Sample response 1

_____

Reason 1	Reason 2
_____	_____
_____	_____
_____	_____
Support _____	**Support** _____
_____	_____

Conclusion: _____
_____

Sample response 2

_____

Reason 1	Reason 2
_____	_____
_____	_____
_____	_____
Support _____	**Support** _____
_____	_____

Conclusion: _____
_____

TOEFL Vocabulary Practice

G. Fill in the blanks with the correct words.

controversy   enthusiastic   instruct   incentive   dismissed

1. Businesses often give money as an _____ for people to work harder.
2. People are becoming more and more _____ about skateboarding.
3. Parents always _____ their children to be polite when they have company.
4. Before the 1920s, women's ideas were often _____ because men thought that they were smarter.
5. In the 1976 Olympics, two African-American runners created a lot of _____ when they chose to wear black gloves while they received their medals.

Test

Step 1

Read the prompt.

Is it better to be the leader of a group or a member of a group? Why?

Step 2

Create an outline for your response.

_____

Reason 1

_____

_____

Support _____

_____

Conclusion: _____

Reason 2

_____

_____

Support _____

_____

Step 3

Write a response using your outline from above.

I think it is better to _____
_____.
I like this option because _____
_____.
But the best part is _____
_____
_____ is the best.

Extension

Work with a partner. Take turns saying your response. Then change partners two more times. Time yourselves!

Your time: _____ seconds   Partner one's time: _____ seconds
Your time: _____ seconds   Partner two's time: _____ seconds
Your time: _____ seconds   Partner three's time: _____ seconds

Integrated

Getting Ready to Speak

A. Learn the words.

Key Vocabulary

boss	the person who supervises or pays employees
double	twice the amount
skip	to miss; to be absent; to not attend
requirement	something that is necessary

TOEFL Vocabulary

sociology	the study of human society
journal	a book or magazine published for studies
shift	a period of work
accumulation	continual growth or addition
investment	a contribution of money or something valuable to get eventual returns

B. Listen to the first part of a conversation. Then answer the questions. Track 69

1. What are the students discussing?
   The students are discussing _____.

2. What does the man have to do?
   The man has _____.

3. What do you think the rest of the conversation will be about?
   I think the rest of the conversation will be about _____
   _____.

4. What do you think the man should do?
   I think the man should _____.

Now practice the questions and answers with a partner.

C. Listen and repeat. Track 70

Practice

A. **Listen to the full conversation and take notes.** Track 71

Man	Woman
• Has _____ _____	• Thinks he _____ _____
• Both school _____ _____	• Recommends that he _____ _____
• Student needs _____ _____	• Thinks of a loan as _____ _____
• Doesn't want _____ _____	• Future job will _____ _____
• Will probably _____ _____	• Should check _____ _____

B. **Use your notes to complete the answers.**

1. Why does the man want to continue his job?
   The man _____
   _____.

2. What are some of the reasons the woman thinks he should quit his job?
   The woman thinks _____
   _____.

Now practice the questions and answers with a partner.

C. **Read the prompt.**

> The students discuss whether the student should keep his job or quit. Describe the reasons for each choice. Then state which you think is the better option.

D. Listen to the sample response and complete the outline. `Track 72`

The conversation is about _____.
  A. Woman's reasons why he should quit his job
    1. School is _____
    2. University is _____
    3. A good education will _____ _____
    _____
  B. Man's reasons to keep his job
    1. Thinks he should _____
    2. Believes he can _____
    3. Doesn't want _____
Conclusion: I think _____
          because _____.

E. Write your own conclusion using the outline from above.

Conclusion: I think _____
because _____.

F. Now work with a partner. Take turns saying your own response using the outline from above.

Your time: _____ seconds   Your partner's time: _____ seconds

G. Fill in the blanks with the correct words.

accumulation	investments	journal	shift	sociology

1. In the Arctic, there is a large ____ _____ of snow every winter.
2. Doctoral students often have their essays published in a _____.
3. Nurses usually have to do _____ work.
4. Good _____ can earn people a lot of money.
5. _____ is the study of people and their societies.

Test

Step 1

Advantages to investing money	Disadvantages to investing money
• It's a good way to _____ _____	• Can't _____ _____
• Can earn _____ _____	• Banks may charge _____ _____
• Will become _____ _____	• Could _____ if _____

Step 2

Read the prompt.

> The students are discussing investments. Describe the advantages and disadvantages of investing money. Then state if you would invest and why?

Step 3

Create an outline for your response.

The conversation is about _____.

    A. The advantages of investing are that

        1. you can _____

        2. it's possible to earn _____

        3. you may become _____

    B. The disadvantages of investing are that

        1. you can't _____

        2. banks may _____

        3. it's possible to _____

Conclusion: I think _____

_____.

Step 4

Write a response using your outline.

The conversation is about _____.
Investing can be good because _____.
In fact, you can _____ and
_____. Some disadvantages are
_____
_____.
I think _____
_____
_____.

Work with a partner. Take turns saying your response. Then change partners two more times. Time yourselves!

Your time: _____ seconds   Partner one's time: _____ seconds
Your time: _____ seconds   Partner two's time: _____ seconds
Your time: _____ seconds   Partner three's time: _____ seconds

Check-up

Fill in the blanks with the correct words.

boss	double	requirement	skip
member	extremely	continue	rarely

1. It's best not to _____ classes.
2. A high TOEFL score is a _____ at many universities.
3. Most people would like to _____ their income.
4. You should always be respectful of your _____.
5. Large animals like deer and lions are _____ seen in big cities.
6. People who win the lottery are _____ lucky.
7. People often choose to _____ learning by going to graduate school after finishing university.
8. It is often difficult and expensive to become a _____ of a country club.

[12] Independent

Getting Ready to Speak

A. Learn the words.

Key Vocabulary

et cetera (etc.)	more examples; and so forth; and others
give in	to accept demands
fit in	to conform well with surroundings
certainly	without doubt

TOEFL Vocabulary

actions	things that somebody does
overwhelm	to affect someone's emotions in a complete way
vocabulary	the words of a language
attribute	to think something is caused by something else
observe	to notice something by watching

B. Read the prompt. Then answer the questions.

Talk about the last thing that you did on impulse.

1. What did you do?
   I _____.

2. How did it make you feel? Why?
   It made me feel _____.

3. What influenced you to do this?
   I did this because _____.

Now practice the questions and answers with a partner.

C. **Listen and repeat.** Track 74

Practice

Prompt 1

A. Read the prompt. Then take turns answering the questions with a partner.

Think about a TV advertisement that you recently saw or heard.

1. What were they advertising?
2. What happened in the advertisement?
3. How did you react to the advertisement?
4. Did you follow the advice of the advertisement? Why or why not?

B. Make a list of people or things that help you to make decisions with your classmates.

_____

_____

_____

_____

Prompt 2

C. Read the prompt. Then complete the answers with your own information.

Talk about what you do before you make a big decision.

Who?	I talk to _____.
How long?	I start making my decision _____.
What?	I get the best information from _____.
Why?	I trust this information because _____.

Now practice your answers with a partner.

D. Make a list of things that you think about before you make a big decision with a partner.

_____

_____

_____

_____

E. Read the prompt. Then underline the phrases you could use in your own response.

Which is more influential in determining your actions, TV or people around you?

Reasons TV or people are influential

- very convincing
- think it will help
- good presentation
- friends enjoy it
- observe its effects
- actions overwhelm me

Sample Response and Outline

F. Now listen to the sample responses and complete the outlines. Track 75

| Sample response 1 | Sample response 2 |

_____

_____

Reason 1
_____
_____
_____

Reason 2
_____
_____
_____

Support _____
_____
_____

Support _____
_____
_____

Conclusion: _____
_____

Reason 1
_____
_____
_____

Reason 2
_____
_____
_____

Support _____
_____
_____

Support _____
_____
_____

Conclusion: _____
_____

TOEFL Vocabulary Practice

G. Fill in the blanks with the correct words.

actions   overwhelm   vocabulary   attribute   observe

1. Many tourists love going to Africa to _____ all the wild animals.
2. Using a big _____ when you speak can make you sound smart.
3. Basketball players often _____ people with their height.
4. The _____ that you take today can have a big effect on tomorrow.
5. Many people _____ pizza to Italy, but it was actually first made by Italians living in New York.

Test

Step 1

Read the prompt.

> Which is more influential in determining your actions, TV or people around you?

Step 2

Create an outline for your response.

_____

Reason 1

_____

_____

Support _____

_____

_____

Reason 2

_____

_____

Support _____

_____

_____

Conclusion: _____

_____

Step 3

Write a response using your outline from above.

I think that _____ are the most influential.
This is because _____
_____.
It is also influential because _____
_____
_____.
_____ are very influential.

Extension

👥 **Work with a partner. Take turns saying your response. Then change partners two more times. Time yourselves!**

Your time: _____ seconds   Partner one's time: _____ seconds
Your time: _____ seconds   Partner two's time: _____ seconds
Your time: _____ seconds   Partner three's time: _____ seconds

Integrated

Getting Ready to Speak

A. Learn the words.

jungle	a tropical forest
shriek	a loud high-pitched sound or scream
meaning	what something means or signifies
bush	a plant made of wood that is much shorter than a tree

territory	land or area
oral	of the mouth
caution	to warn
apparent	clearly understood
evaluation	an assessment of the value of something

B. Listen to the first part of a lecture. Then answer the questions. `Track 76`

1. For many years, scientists thought that only humans could do what?
   Scientists thought that only humans _____.

2. What did scientists who disagreed begin to do?
   Scientists who disagreed began to _____.

3. What do you think the scientists found out?
   I think the scientists found out that _____.

Now practice the questions and answers with a partner.

C. Listen and repeat. `Track 77`

Practice

A. **Listen to the full lecture and take notes.** `Track 78`

- The vervet monkey also uses verbal communication.
- They live _____
- They have many _____
- The vervet has a loud _____
- Scientists analyzed _____
- They are used to _____
- Each shriek _____
- One shriek means _____
- Another shriek means _____
- It is important _____
- Vervets have a vocabulary _____
- It seems humans and vervets both use verbal communication.

B. **Use your notes to complete the answers.**

1. What did scientists learn from vervet monkeys?
   They learned that _____
   _____.

2. Why do vervets need to be able to communicate?
   They need to communicate because _____
   _____.

Now practice the questions and answers with a partner.

C. **Read the prompt.**

> The professor talked about the verbal communication with the vervet monkeys. Using points and examples from the lecture, talk about how and why vervets communicate.

D. Listen to the sample response and complete the outline. `Track 79`

The lecture is about _____.

    A. The vervet

        1. has _____ _____

        2. lives _____ _____

    B. Vervets make _____

    C. The shrieks are used to _____

        1. One shriek means _____

        2. Another shriek means _____

    D. The vervet must run to _____

    E. The vervet has a vocabulary of _____

Conclusion: Humans and vervets both seem to use verbal communication.

E. Now work with a partner. Take turns saying your own response using the outline from above.

Your time: _____ seconds   Your partner's time: _____ seconds

F. Fill in the blanks with the correct words.

    territory   oral   caution   apparent   evaluations

1. Many language tests now require an _____ test to make sure that people can speak the language well.

2. Good bosses receive good comments on employee _____.

3. Russia has more _____ than any other country in the world.

4. Teachers and parents always _____ students about drugs.

5. From a very young age, it was very _____ that Mozart would become a brilliant musician.

Test

Step 1

Listen to the lecture and take notes. **Track 80**

- Vervets' verbal communication is difficult to understand.
- Many people do not hear _____
- Some scientists thought vervets _____
- Scientists used computers to _____
- The shrieks were _____
- They first learned that shrieks were _____
- Scientists put _____
- They played the tapes and watched _____
- Scientists want to study _____
- Other monkeys live _____
- Vervets' are small, smart, and _____
- Scientists have learned a lot from _____

Step 2

Read the prompt.

> The professor describes how scientists learned that vervets used verbal communication. Using points and examples from the lecture, describe how the scientists learned this.

Step 3

Create an outline for your response.

The lecture is about vervets' verbal communication.
- A. Difficult to understand
    1. Many people could not hear _____
    2. Scientists did not think vervets could _____
- B. Used Computers
    1. Computers _____
    2. Final evaluation showed _____
- C. Scientists studied the meanings by
    1. Putting _____
    2. Watching _____
- D. Studying
    1. Other monkeys are difficult to study because _____
    2. Vervets are easy _____

Scientists have learned _____.

Step 4

Write a response using your outline.

> The lecture is about _____.
> Vervets are difficult to understand. Many people _____
> _____.
> Some scientists _____.
> The scientists used computers to _____
> _____.
> Scientists learned the meanings of the shrieks by _____.
> They want to study other monkeys, but _____
> _____.
> They have taught _____.

Extension

Work with a partner. Take turns saying your response. Then change partners two more times. Time yourselves!

Your time: _____ seconds   Partner one's time: _____ seconds

Your time: _____ seconds   Partner two's time: _____ seconds

Your time: _____ seconds   Partner three's time: _____ seconds

Check-up

Fill in the blanks with the correct words.

jungle	shriek	meaning	bushes
etc.	gave in	fit in	certainly

1. Tigers are the one of the most scary animals in the _____.

2. Blueberries grow on _____, while bananas grow on trees.

3. It is common for people to _____ when they are surprised.

4. Many people often wonder what the _____ of life is.

5. All parents _____ want their children to grow up to be successful.

6. After years of fighting, Protestants and Catholics finally _____ and agreed to peace.

7. Westerners with blonde hair and blue eyes often do not _____ when traveling through Asia.

8. When moving to a new home, you have to pack your clothes, clean your house, move your things, _____.

[Review 2]

Step 1

Listen to the prompt.

> Some people think it is better to go to university and study before getting a job. Others think you should get a job instead of going to university. What do you think is better? Why?

Step 2

Create an outline for your response.

_____

First reason

_____

_____

Like to

_____

_____

Second reason

_____

_____

_____

_____

Conclusion: _____

_____

Step 3

Write a response using your outline from above.

> I think it is best to _____ when I graduate high school.
> I would like to _____ because
> _____.
> I think this is the best idea because I will _____
> _____.

 Work with a partner. Take turns saying your response. Then change partners two more times. Time yourselves!

Your time: _____ seconds	Partner one's time: _____ seconds
Your time: _____ seconds	Partner two's time: _____ seconds
Your time: _____ seconds	Partner three's time: _____ seconds

Step 1

Read the passage.

> ### Sign Language
>
> Adults and children who are deaf and hard of hearing use sign language. It is a language that uses hand movement and body language instead of spoken words. Sign language is used internationally, but it varies from country to country. People often take sign language classes at a university. Becoming a translator is one of the options for someone looking for a career using sign language.

Step 2

Listen to the lecture and take notes. Track 81

Sign Language

- Used by _____

- A language that uses _____

- Dates back to _____

- Varies _____

- Classes are offered at _____

- People who study sign language are usually _____

  _____

- A good career is _____

- The most common sign is _____

- Libraries and bookstores have _____

Step 3

Read the prompt.

> The professor is talking about sign language. Explain why people use sign language and what career choices are available for people who want to use sign language.

Step 4

Create an outline for your response.

The passage and lecture are about _____.

    A. Sign language

        1. started in _____

        2. is used by _____ _____

    B. Universities offer classes if _____

       _____

    C. A career using sign language is _____

    D. The most common sign is _____

    E. Bookstores and libraries have _____

       _____

Step 5

Write a response using your outline from above.

>   The passage and lecture are about _____. Sign language started in the _____. It is used by people _____. Often universities offer classes if _____. _____ is a career option for someone who wants to pursue sign language. The most common universal sign in sign language is for _____. Bookstores and libraries are great places to find _____.

👤👤 **Work with a partner. Take turns saying your response. Then change partners two more times. Time yourselves!**

Your time: _____ seconds   Partner one's time: _____ seconds

Your time: _____ seconds   Partner two's time: _____ seconds

Your time: _____ seconds   Partner three's time: _____ seconds

Step 1

Listen to the conversation and take notes. Track 82

Man	Woman
• Asks woman _____ _____ • _____ by college applications • Thinking about _____ or joining _____ • Doesn't want to _____ traveling • Still plans to _____ _____	• The woman is working on _____ _____ • Asks _____ • Thought he was interested in _____ _____ • _____ will give chance to travel • Wishes him good luck

Step 2

Read the prompt.

> The male student expresses that he is not sure if he wants to attend university. Describe the advantages and disadvantages of not going to university. Then state what you would prefer.

Step 3

Create an outline for your response.

The conversation is about _____

_____.

    A. The student must choose whether _____

        _____

    B. Not attending university

        1. Can join _____

        2. Or _____

    C. If he goes to university

        1. He can _____

        2. He is too _____ to make a decision.

Conclusion: I would prefer _____

_____.

Step 4

Write a response using your outline.

The conversation is about _____
_____.
The student must choose whether _____
_____. If he does not attend
university, he can join the _____ or _____. If he
goes to university, he can _____ and still go to school.

Work with a partner. Take turns saying your response. Then change partners two more times. Time yourselves!

Your time: _____ seconds   Partner one's time: _____ seconds
Your time: _____ seconds   Partner two's time: _____ seconds
Your time: _____ seconds   Partner three's time: _____ seconds

Step 1

Read the prompt.

There are lots of types of music. Some people like to listen to hip hop or pop music because they can dance to it. Some people like to listen to classical or opera music because it is relaxing. What type of music do you like or dislike? Why?

Step 2

Create an outline for your response.

_____

First reason

_____

_____

Better because

_____

_____

Second reason

_____

_____

_____

_____

Conclusion: _____

_____

Step 3

Write a response using your outline.

I think people should listen to _____.

It is usually a lot more enjoyable to _____

_____.

This allows people to _____

_____.

_____ music is _____.

Work with a partner. Take turns saying your response. Then change partners two more times. Time yourselves!

Your time: _____ seconds

Your time: _____ seconds

Your time: _____ seconds

Partner one's time: _____ seconds

Partner two's time: _____ seconds

Partner three's time: _____ seconds

Speaking Feedback and Evaluation Form

The response...	0	1	2	3	4
CONTENT addresses the question or prompt well					
has relevant details					
connects ideas clearly					
LANGUAGE uses accurate grammar					
uses appropriate vocabulary					
has fluent speech					
has clear pronunciation					

Total: _____ /28

Basic Skills for the
TOEFL® iBT 2

Edaan Getzel
Tanya Yaunish

Speaking

Transcript & Answer Key

Transcript

[Unit 1]

Page 15

C

M: My favorite movie is *Mary Poppins*. I first saw this movie when I was a young child. I like this movie so much because it has great music and a happy ending.

Page 17

F

Sample answer 1

M: The movie *Life is Beautiful* had a positive influence on my life. The movie is a story about a Jewish man from Italy. He and his family are taken from their home during World War II. They endure many hardships. But, the man never gives up hope. He teaches his son to overcome hardships. He does this by showing him beauty in the world. Because of this movie, I try to see beauty every day in the world.

Sample answer 2

W: A book about the musician Mozart had a positive influence on my life. The specific book I like is about all that he accomplished at a young age. It describes his beautiful and authentic music. His music changed people's lives. I am trying to be just like him. I am learning to play the piano and also learning to write music. Because of this book, I hope to one day have as great a cultural impact as Mozart did.

Integrated

Page 19

C

W: The announcement says that buses will not stop at the Preston Road bus stop. Therefore, students should begin using the Davis Boulevard stop. I think the conversation will be about what students think of the bus routes changing.

Page 20

B

M: Did you hear the school is closing the Preston Road bus stop?
W: Yes. I am not happy about it at all. This bus route change is terrible for me!
M: Why? Do you live near the Preston Road bus stop?
W: No. I live in the apartments near campus, but I use that bus route because I like to shop at SaveMart.
M: Oh. Well, you can still take the bus to Davis Boulevard and walk to SaveMart. It's not that far.
W: It's not far, but after shopping, I would have to walk back to Davis Boulevard with several heavy bags of groceries!
M: I see.
W: Now it will be a lot more difficult for students to shop at SaveMart. We will all have to shop at the more expensive stores near campus. This is terrible!
M: But the university doesn't have the money to keep that bus route open. What can it do? It has no other options.
W: The University should spend less money on its football team and more money on its buses. That's what I think it should do.

Page 21

D

W: The woman is not happy about the bus route change. She thinks this change in bus routes is an inconvenience because now it is more difficult to take the bus to SaveMart to get groceries. She also thinks the bus route change is an inconvenience because now students will have to shop at the more expensive stores near campus. She thinks the university should spend less money on the football team and more on the bus system. The man doesn't think it is an inconvenience. He thinks the university doesn't have the money to keep the bus stop going.

Page 22

Step 2

W: Did you hear the city is closing Kirby Road?

M: Yeah. It is going to make my walk to school a lot longer.

W: I know what you mean. I live in an apartment north of Kirby Road, and I walk to school, too. I will have to leave my apartment at least fifteen minutes earlier than usual to get to class on time. It will be an inconvenience for us, but I'm glad they're finally repairing Kirby Road.

M: You're glad?

W: Sure. That road has big holes in it. When my parents came to visit me, they had to drive down that road; the holes were terrible.

M: I think they needed to repair the road too, but they should at least let us walk through the area. We are all adults. We won't get hurt walking to school through the work area.

W: No, I think they did the right thing closing the whole area. Better safe than sorry.
Besides, a longer walk to class means more exercise. Maybe we'll all be in better shape by the end of the semester!

[Unit 2]

Independent

Page 25

C

W: My father is a businessman. He works in an office. He has worked there for fifteen years.

Page 27

F

Sample answer 1

W: The most important thing when choosing a career is finding a job that pays a sufficient salary. Everybody needs to have money to buy food and pay for a home. It is also important to ensure that you can take care of your family. Many people who want to be artists or singers often find it very hard to pay their rent. Bankers and doctors, though, don't have this problem. They have enough money to care for themselves and their family.

Sample answer 2

M: The most important thing when choosing a career is having a job that allows you to be creative. A creative job allows people to be much more emotional and involved in their work. This makes them more satisfied. Those with boring jobs only go to work because it is their duty to go. They rarely give their best effort. I think if you have to work, do something that makes you happy, and do your best!

Integrated

Page 29

C

M: The passage is about Art Deco, which was one of the most popular styles of design in the 1920s. Many Art Deco buildings were built using stainless steel and glass. I think that the lecture will be about Art Deco architecture.

B

W: Art Deco was a very popular design movement worldwide in the 1920s. It began in France at the start of the 1900s. It was really popular in America. It can still be seen on buildings there today. It was used in architecture and interior design. Designers used modern ideas at their disposal to come up with new ideas. Things like African art, and new technologies like ocean liners and the radio inspired them. It had very strong links with the machine age. The style was all about looking good. It did not have any other motives. It used many zigzags and jumbled shapes. One of the best known Art Deco buildings is the Chrysler building. It is a skyscraper with a large spire and a sunburst pattern. It is made from stainless steel and glass. Most of the buildings were made in this way. The style was also used in other places. It could even be found on ladies shoes and cars at the time. Art Deco has come and gone many times since the 1920s. It is still popular today. It can be seen in the style of many cartoons and movies.

Page 31

D

M: The lecture and the passage were about architecture and Art Deco. Art Deco was a popular design style in the 1920s. It was a very modern style that used old and modern ideas for inspiration. It was all about making the inside and outside of buildings look good. It was also used in many other places. Buildings often had spires and sunburst patterns. Many were made using stainless steel and glass. All of these things can be seen on the Chrysler building. It is a famous Art Deco skyscraper.

Page 32

Step 2

M: One of the best known Art Deco buildings worldwide is the Empire State building. It has been in many movies, like King Kong. It has 6,500 windows and looks like it has vertical stripes going down it. It is 102 stories tall and was built in 1930. It only took sixteen months to build. This was because of the many technical advances in building at the time. When it was finished it was called the eighth wonder of the world. It is unlike some other Art Deco buildings. It does not have any curves or sunbursts on it. The top of the building does have a common Art Deco shape. This is called a ziggurat. It is like a pyramid where each floor gets smaller than the one below it. One of the diverse Art Deco influences was Egyptian architecture. King Tutankhamen's tomb was discovered in the 1920s. Soon after, designers found this new style at their disposal. A lot of the building's interior was decorated with marble and polished wood. Most styles before Art Deco only looked backwards. The Art Deco style mixed old and new ideas to look to the future.

[Unit 3]

Independent

Page 35

C

M: Every day I use my cell phone. I use it all the time. It helps me by allowing me to always be in contact with my friends and family.

Page 37

F

Sample answer 1

M: I think that the greatest invention is plastic. Plastic has had a profound effect on how we make things that we use every day. It is much lighter, cheaper, and easier to shape than traditional materials like wood and metal. It is also very versatile. We use plastic in everything. We use it in computers, cars, and tools that we use in hospitals. Our lives depend on plastic, so I think it is the greatest invention.

Sample answer 2

W: I think that the airplane is the greatest invention. The airplane lets us go anywhere in the world. We used to travel by boat, but the airplane gave us a superior way to complete our journey. The airplane lets us visit far off places and it also moves products from one place in the world to another place very quickly. The airplane is crucial to our daily lives, so I think it is the greatest invention.

Integrated

Page 39

B

M: Hi, Jen. What's wrong?
W: I have a problem and I don't know what to do.
M: What is it?
W: I saw one of my classmates cheating. He was copying from a student who took this course last semester.

C

W: The students are discussing the woman's problem. She saw one of her classmates cheating and she doesn't know what to do. I think the rest of conversation will be about what she should do. I think she should tell her teacher immediately.

Page 40

A

M: Hi. Jen, What's wrong?
W: I have a problem and I don't know what to do.
M: What is it?
W: I saw one of my classmates cheating. He was copying from a student who took this course last semester.
M: That's terrible. Are you sure he was cheating? It would be a shame if you had made a mistake.
W: I really don't want to accuse someone if he is innocent, but I'm sure that's what I saw.
M: The university's policy on plagiarism is very strict. Students who cheat are expelled from the university.
W: That's why I'm not sure if I should tell someone.
M: You know that cheating is wrong. He has deceived the professor and he should be punished.
W: But, I don't want to be responsible for him being kicked out of school. I would feel so bad.
M: I think you should tell your professor. It's the right thing to do.
W: I don't think it would help anyone if I tell the teacher. I wish I could forget about it.
M: You can't. It's not fair to the students who work hard to get good grades.
W: Maybe he had a good reason for resorting to cheating. I should talk to him.
M: Well, it's your choice. I hope you make the right one.

Page 41

D

W: The conversation is about whether the student should tell her professor that she saw another student cheating. The man thinks that she should tell her professor because cheating is wrong. It's not fair to all the other students. He should be punished and expelled from school. The woman wants to forget about it. She doesn't want to be responsible for the student being kicked out. She thinks he may have a good reason for cheating. I think that she shouldn't tell her professor. Copying one assignment isn't so terrible. Maybe the student was too busy with his other school work. Also, he could have had some personal problems. I think she should be more understanding of him and check why he did it before she tells a professor.

Page 42

Step 1

W: Hi, Tom. Do you have a minute?
M: Sure, Julie. What do you need?

W: I was wondering if you could help me. I know you've taken this course before and I need some help with my mid-term paper. Do you think I could look at yours to help me get started?

M: I'd like to help you, but isn't that plagiarism? I really don't want to get into trouble for deceiving the professor.

W: I understand that, but I won't copy your essay. It's just that I have no time this week to work on mine. I have to resort to this in order to pass the course. If I could use a part of your paper, it would really help me. Then, the next time you need help in geography, I'll give you one of my papers.

M: That sounds like a good idea, but I'm still worried. I don't want anyone to accuse us of cheating.

W: I wouldn't worry. It's not against the school's policy to help each other. Anyway, no one will know. It will be a secret between us and we'll both benefit.

M: It still seems a little dangerous. I need to think about it before I make my decision.

[Unit 4]

Independent

Page 45

C

W: I respect my cousin Jessie. I respect my cousin because she is kind and diligent and because she always thinks of ways to help other people. I want to be like my cousin because she is loved and respected by so many people.

Page 47

F

Sample response 1

W: I respect my grandfather the most. He was such a great man. As a child he was very poor. But he overcame this because he was very diligent. Even though he worked hard, he never neglected his family. He always made time for them. In addition, he always gave me great advice whenever I had a problem. His wisdom always helped me find an answer to my problems. I love and respect my grandfather so much.

Sample response 2

M: I respect Bono, the lead singer of the rock band U2, the most. He plays wonderful music, but I respect him more for the charity work that he does. Bono is concerned with the welfare of everyone in the world. He is trying hard to get rid of poverty all around the world. He often works for charities to help poor African countries. Bono simultaneously makes great music and helps many people, so I think everyone should respect Bono.

Integrated

Page 49

B

M: Today we are going to discuss a very special plant. Like all plants, it has leaves, roots, and stems. This plant is different, though, because it is a carnivore. This plant is called the Venus Flytrap.

C

M: The lecture is about a very special plant called a Venus Flytrap. It is different because it is a carnivore. I think the plant has to do this because it is really hungry.

Page 50

A

M: Today we are going to discuss a very special plant. Like all plants, it has leaves, roots, and stems. This plant is different, though, because it is a carnivore. This plant is called the Venus Flytrap. These plants don't eat meat like steak or chicken. Instead, they eat small insects. The main factor causing their unusual diet is deficient soil. Eating insects gives them more nutrients to become bigger, stronger, and healthier.

In addition to insects, these plants also need air and water to live.

The Venus Flytrap is green. It has round flat leaves with long green fingers on the end of each leaf. Each leaf has a series of small hairs. When an insect stimulates the hair, the leaf snaps shut around the insect. The plant then emits juices that kill the insect. After this, the plant spends five to twelve days digesting the juices. Once it is finished, it takes twelve hours for the leaf to open back up. The Flytrap must be careful, though, about what it eats. If the insect is too big, the plant can become sick and die. If the bug is too small, the Flytrap will not get enough food.

Page 51

D

W: This lecture is about a carnivorous plant called the Venus Flytrap. It eats insects. The main factor for this is that they grow in places with deficient soil. Eating insects gives them nutrients. This helps them to be strong and healthy. They also need air and water to live.
The Venus Flytrap has round flat leaves with fingers on them. Each leaf has a series of hairs. When insects touch the hairs, the leaf snaps shut around the insect. The plant emits juices that kill the insect. The plant then digests the juices. However, the Flytrap must be careful. If it eats something that is too big or too small, it can die. Flytraps are a very special plant.

Page 52

Step 1

W: There are carnivorous plants throughout the world. However, all carnivorous plants live in areas that have deficient soil. All carnivorous plants also get a lot of sun and water. But different plants catch insects in different ways. There are a series of ways that carnivorous plants catch insects. Plants like the Venus Flytrap use snap traps. This means that when the leaf is stimulated, it snaps shut.

Another kind of plant catches insects with glue. These plants emit a glue like juice from the leaves. When insects touch the leaf, they get stuck and can't move.

A third kind of plant is called a Lobster Trap. These are usually found in the sea. These work because it is easy to go inside the plant. But it is very difficult for the insect to go back out. The plant uses a series of hairs to tell the insects which way to go.

The final kind of carnivorous plant is shaped like a very tall bowl. The plant emits juices that insects want to eat. So the insect comes to eat the juices, and it falls into the bowl. The walls of the plant are very high, so the insect can't climb out. There are many ways carnivorous plants catch their food.

[Unit 5]

Independent

Page 55

C

M: I recently celebrated Chuseok. For Chuseok, I helped my family make the traditional dish, songpyon. I enjoyed the holiday because I got to see all of my cousins, aunts, and uncles.

Page 57

F

Sample response 1

M: My favorite holiday is the Jewish holiday of Rosh Hashona. It is a celebration of the Jewish New Year. Every year, my family gathers for a dinner. The following day, we all go to a ceremony where we pray and listen to stories about the Jewish religion. I have to admit that the ceremony is often boring, but I endure it because sometimes there is a really great story. However, my favorite part of Rosh Hashona is that I get a day off school!

Sample response 2

W: My favorite holiday in America is Memorial Day. It is a national holiday when we honor all of the men and women who died while fighting wars for America. While this is sad, most people can't resist the fact that Memorial Day is the beginning of summer. Everyone has barbeque parties in their yards. Swimming pools open for the summer. Most importantly, Memorial Day means that the school summer vacation will start in a few weeks!

Integrated

Page 59

C

W: The announcement says that the "Beginning of Term Picnic" will be held on Friday at 12:30. There will be live entertainment and games with prizes. I think the conversation will be about the students' interest in the picnic.

Page 60

B

W: Hey, John. Did you hear about the picnic? It sounds like fun.
M: I think it sounds like a terrible idea.
W: Really? But there will be food, games, entertainment. What's wrong with that?
M: Well, did you think about who is paying for this? Our tuition fees help pay for these events. I think there are much better ways to use our money. The university should use our money only on essential things. I mean we need new computers for the library.
W: I guess that's true.
M: Also, it's such a waste of time. We came here to learn, not to eat and play games. We're university students, not children.
W: Yes, but we can have fun sometimes. I think that's important, too.
M: Honestly, I don't. We can have fun on our own time. I don't know why the university has to impose this kind of activity on us. Not only do they spend our money on it but my older sister went last year and she thought it was terrible.
W: Well, if you feel that way, maybe you shouldn't go.
M: I don't think I will. In fact, I'm going to write a letter to protest how they use our money.

Page 61

D

M: The man thinks that the picnic is a bad idea. He thinks it's a waste of time and money. He thinks the university should spend the money on more essential things. He says the library needs new computers. He won't go to the picnic.

Page 62

Step 2

W: Steve, are you busy on Wednesday morning?
M: No, I'm not. Why?
W: Well, I don't want to impose, but could you drive me to the campus events office.
M: Sure, what time?
W: About 6 a.m.
M: Six? Why do you need to go there so early?
W: Well, I need to get a ticket for a rock concert.
M: A rock concert? That will be expensive!
W: No, it's free. But I have to pick up a voucher on Wednesday morning. You should come with me to the concert. It's on Wednesday at 4 p.m. in the gymnasium.
M: Honestly, I'd love to, but I have class then.
W: I know you don't want to ruin your perfect attendance record, but you must come. It's going to be filmed for a music video. We could be famous!

M: Ha ha! Well, maybe I could go. What if I miss something important in class, though?

W: Just stop protesting and say yes. I'm sure you'll have a lot of fun.

M: OK, I'll drive you to the office on Wednesday and I will get a voucher, too! I know you won't be satisfied until I say yes.

W: Yes! I knew I could persuade you!

[Unit 6]

Independent

Page 65

C

W: I live in Taipei. My city is famous for our beautiful building, Taipei 101. People should visit my city because they can eat all the great food and go to the top of one of the tallest buildings in the world.

Page 67

F

Sample response 1

W: The best city that I have been to is Sydney. Everyone is so nice, and it is perhaps the cleanest city that I have ever visited. Sydney also has beautiful architecture like the Opera House and the Harbor Bridge. Also, everyone there is fluent in English, so I can communicate easily. Finally, Sydney has beautiful scenery, especially the beaches where I learned to surf and relax in the sun. One day, I would like to immigrate to Sydney.

Sample response 2

M: The best city that I have been to is Istanbul. It is such an amazing city with so much history. The buildings there are so old but still really beautiful. There is also a great feeling in the city. It is really informal, but it also has a lot of energy. The people who reside there are very friendly and are always willing to help. But the best part of the city is the food. I love Istanbul.

Integrated

Page 69

C

M: The passage is about volcanoes and geology, which is the science of the solid matter that makes up the Earth. It looks at rocks and soils. When molten rock reaches the Earth's surface, it explodes through the ground. I think that the lecture will be about volcanoes and what causes them.

Page 70

B

W: OK, so you all know what a volcano is. It is an opening in the Earth's surface that lets out molten rock, ash, and gas from below. The explosions can be hazardous to all life nearby. They can come in many shapes and sizes. Most of them are on the seabed but there are many on land, too. They can cause mountains to appear over time. This is because the molten rock cools and becomes hard over time. This happens repeatedly. Over time, the rock builds up higher. This is what causes the mountains to form. A volcano can be caused by the movement of plates on the Earth's surface. It can also happen where the Earth's crust is thin. This is called a "hotspot." It can be seen on islands like Hawaii. There are many active volcanoes there. A volcano is called "active" when it erupts often. It is called "dormant" when it is not erupting. And it is called "extinct" when it has not erupted in a long time and is not expected to again. Many people argue over these words because a volcano may not have exploded for thousands of years but it does not mean that it will not again.

D

M: The lecture and passage were about volcanoes and where they can occur. Volcanoes happen when molten rock, ash, and gases escape from beneath the Earth's crust. This molten rock is called magma. When the rock, ash, and gases escape it happens in a big explosion. Volcanic eruptions can take place on the seabed or on land. These eruptions can cause mountains to form. When the molten rock cools down, it becomes hard and can build up mountains over time. They can happen when plates on the Earth's surface move or in places where the crust is thin. They have different names depending on how often they erupt.

Step 2

M: One of the best known hotspots in the world is not on the seabed, like in Hawaii. It is thought to be under Yellowstone Park in the US. There are several craters there. These are called calderas. The Yellowstone Caldera is called a supervolcano. When it erupts, volcanic matter can change all of the land around it. Such a climactic event can even affect the weather all around the world. It has not erupted for over half a million years. And it is not expected to erupt in the near future. It is not dormant though. Deep under the park is a large body of magma. It is covered in hot water and steam. This often escapes to the surface in what are called geysers. This is where boiling water and steam repeatedly shoot up into the air from the ground. There are over 300 of them in the park. The area is so active that the land in the park can rise and fall by up to 1cm every year. The land in the park is now covered in trees and is filled with animals. But below the surface lies tons of hot molten rock.

[Review 1]

Integrated 1

Step 2

M: Hey Megan, are you going to attend the graduation ball next weekend?
W: I hope so, but it depends on if the administration gives me permission . . . they said they would let me know by the end of this week.
M: I don't understand. Why do you need permission to go? You are graduating, aren't you?
W: Well last week I was told I do not have enough credits to graduate this spring.
M: Seriously?
W: Yeah, they said I am missing a technical writing class and a few math credits. The dean of the college said I could go to summer school and receive my diploma at the end of summer, but I would miss having a graduation ceremony. Another option would be to come back in the fall and complete my classes. I'm still trying to figure out how I neglected to take those classes.
M: What a huge inconvenience to have to go to school all summer. However, that sounds way better than coming back in the fall.
W: Having said that, since the graduation ball is only for graduating seniors, the administration wasn't sure if that included me. I think it might be a school policy.
M: I'm sorry to hear about this. Hmmm . . . well if they decide against you going, you should come hangout with me, I'm not going; it's way too expensive.
W: That sounds like a plan Sam, but I hope I can go. It is supposed to be really fun.
M: Give me a call when you find out. See ya later Megan!
W: Bye Sam.

Page 78

Step 1

W: Botany is the study of plants. There are several different ways to categorize plants. One of those ways is to categorize them by their life span. Most flowering plants fall into one of three categories. Annuals, biennials and perennials are the three categories. A few examples of annuals are petunias and snapdragons. They usually bloom between late spring and early fall. If the annual germinates before it dies then the seeds have a chance to come up in the following spring. Biennials produce leaves in the first year and in the second year produces flowers and seeds. Perennials last more than two years, annuals last no longer than a year and biennials last no more than two years. Trees and shrubs are usually perennials. Perennials and biennials are more likely to endure cold climates because they go dormant in the wintertime. For example pine trees and holly bushes are perennials. Annuals are less likely to survive cold weather.

[Unit 7]

Independent

Page 81

C

W: The last place I traveled to was Paris. I went with my friends Dave and Dan. My vacation could have been better if I were able to speak French.

Page 83

F

Sample response 1

M: Traveling alone is much better than traveling with a tour group. Traveling by yourself allows you to travel whichever route you want. You can act upon whichever impulses you have. When traveling in a group you always have to stay with the group even if the group does something that you think is boring and a waste of time. Tour groups often stop at souvenir stands for shopping. I hate shopping, so I always prefer to travel alone.

Sample response 2

W: Traveling with a tour group is much better than traveling alone. When you are with a group you are never lonely. There is always someone to talk to. In addition, traveling on a tour ensures that you will see all of the great things on your vacation. Your tour guide will also decide an appropriate amount of time to investigate each site. Finally, because there are more people, traveling in a group can often be cheaper than traveling alone.

Integrated

Page 85

B

M: Hi! You look frustrated. What are you doing?
W: I'm just trying to schedule my classes for next quarter. It's not going very well.
M: Really? What's wrong?
W: Well, I really want to take this anthropology lecture. The professor is very famous and the syllabus looks great. I know I would learn a lot.
M: So, what's the problem?
W: The class is every Tuesday and Thursday evening, which is when I have basketball practice.

C

W: The students are discussing the woman's scheduling problem. The woman has basketball practice at the same time as an anthropology class. I think the conversation will be about choosing between the class and basketball practice. I think she should choose the class.

Page 86

A

M: Hi! You look frustrated. What are you doing?

W: I'm just trying to schedule my classes for next quarter. It's not going very well.

M: Really? What's wrong?

W: Well, I really want to take this anthropology lecture. The professor is very famous and the syllabus looks great. I know I would learn a lot.

M: So, what's the problem?

W: The class is every Tuesday and Thursday evening, which is when I have basketball practice.

M: Is that important? I think that academics are more important than sports. You came to university to study, not play. You should quit basketball.

W: But, basketball is my passion. I've been playing for so long. If I want to qualify for the national team, I have to keep working at it.

M: What about this anthropology course? You still need a science credit for your degree and I know that you loved the last course you took.

W: That's true. However, I came to this university on a basketball scholarship and my coach told us that we can't have more than three absences per quarter if we want to stay on the team.

M: I guess you'll have to choose which is more important for your future.

W: I wish I knew what to do.

Page 87

D

M: The conversation is about the woman's schedule. She wants to take a course but she has basketball practice at the same time. There are many reasons to take the course. The teacher is very famous and the woman would learn a lot. Second, she needs science credits to graduate. Also, she really likes anthropology. However, there are also reasons to go to basketball practice. It is her passion and she has been playing for a long time. She has to practice because she wants to play for the national team. She also has a basketball scholarship. I think she should quit basketball. Her classes are much more important for her future. She needs good classes to get a good job.

Page 88

Step 1

W: Hi, Matt. Are you coming to my birthday party? We're going out for dinner and then to a movie. The movie we're going to is called, *The Passion of Soldiers*.

M: Sure, when is it?

W: Tomorrow night.

M: Tomorrow. That's too bad. I won't be able to make it because I've got other plans.

W: My birthday only comes once a year. What could be more important?

M: I'm the assistant coach of my little brother's soccer team. We have a very important qualifying game tomorrow. I have to be there.

W: If you're the assistant, there must be another coach. I'm sure it won't be a problem if you skipped. No one will notice.

M: My brother will definitely notice my absence. He really depends on me and I don't want to let him down.

W: That's really too bad. A lot of our friends from high school are going to be there. I'm sure they'll be upset that you weren't there.

M: I guess they will. Of course I'd like to see them too. It would be a lot of fun. However, I should keep my promise. I can't decide right now.

W: Hopefully I'll see you tomorrow.

M: Yeah. Either way, I hope you have a happy birthday tomorrow.

W: Thanks.

[Unit 8]

Independent

Page 91

C

W: I normally start studying for a test a week before the exam. I prepare for my test by reading over my class notes and underlining the important areas. I normally feel excited before taking a test.

Page 93

F

Sample response 1

W: I always prefer to study at home rather than at school. When the school day is over, I am always keen to go home. I never want to extend my time at school any longer than I must. In addition, if I were to stay at school, I anticipate my friends would distract me from my preparation. At home, it is quiet with very little to do, so I am able to focus much more on my studies.

Sample response 2

M: I think that studying for tests at school is better than studying at home. Inevitably, something will be unclear, so I can always ask my teacher or classmates for help. In addition, all the books that are needed for the class curriculum are available to me. This lets me answer any questions that I might have on the night before the test. Even though I might have to stay late at school, I never regret studying at school.

Integrated

Page 95

B

M: OK, class. So there are many brilliant writers who lived in England in the 1800s. Bronte, Wordsworth, and Wells all created new characters that are still remembered. But the most famous of all the characters is Sherlock Holmes.

C

M: The lecture is mainly about Sherlock Holmes. The authors, Bronte, Wordsworth, and Wells, all created characters that are still remembered. I think the professor will discuss why Sherlock Holmes is so famous.

Page 96

A

M: OK, class. So there are many brilliant writers who lived in England in the 1800s. Bronte, Wordsworth, and Wells all created new characters that are still remembered. But the most famous of all the characters is Sherlock Holmes. Sir Arthur Conan Doyle created Sherlock Holmes.

Holmes was a detective who lived in London. Holmes was a brilliant man. He was able to analyze vague clues very well. This helped him to predict what happened. He was almost always right. Holmes was able to do this by using his own approach. He would get rid of as many explanations as possible. The last explanation would implicate someone. His friend and partner was Dr. Watson. Watson would help Holmes find the clues. Holmes's main enemy was Professor Moriarty. Moriarty was often doing bad things. Holmes always worked to stop his bad schemes. Holmes was often seen smoking a pipe. He is also usually shown wearing a strange hat. Many people think that the hat and pipe make him look smart.

There are sixty novels and short stories with Sherlock Holmes. People still read his stories. After, some people meet to talk about him. Sherlock Holmes is the most famous detective of all time.

Page 97

D

W: The lecture is about Sherlock Holmes. Sir Arthur Conan Doyle created Holmes. Sherlock Holmes was a brilliant detective. Holmes was able to analyze vague clues very well. This let him predict what was going to happen. He was usually correct. To do this he used his own approach. He always got rid of any explanation he thought was not true. The last explanation left usually implicated someone. Holmes's friend's name was Dr. Watson. His main enemy was Professor Moriarty. Moriarty always had bad schemes. Holmes often wore a strange hat and smoked a pipe. Even though Holmes was written in the 1800s, people still read about him. Then they meet and talk about the stories.

Page 98

Step 1

W: OK, so the brilliant detective Sherlock Holmes was created by Arthur Conan Doyle. Doyle himself was also a brilliant man. He led a very interesting life. Doyle was born in Edinburgh, Scotland. He went to university to become a doctor. He had to analyze clues in the body as a doctor. This helped him predict why someone was sick. Holmes acted in the same way. Doyle wrote his first Sherlock Holmes story in 1882. It was called *A Study in Scarlet*. People loved his first story. So, he wrote more. These stories made Doyle very famous. He used his fame to help others. He helped people who were wrongly implicated of crimes. He helped them become free. Later he tried to run for parliament. He tried two times. Both times he lost. He also played soccer on a team.

It is a little bit vague how Doyle got the idea for Sherlock Holmes. People say that Holmes is based on one of Doyle's professors in university. Holmes also said that he loved to read Edgar Allen Poe. He loved Poe's detective character named C. Auguste Dupin. Sherlock Holmes was a brilliant detective. The man who created Holmes was an equally brilliant man.

[Unit 9]

Independent

Page 101

C

M: The most prominent university in my country is Harvard University. It is located in a big city with many other universities. I don't want to go to this university because I want to go to a university that is closer to my home.

Page 103

F

Sample response 1

M: I would hesitate to go to school in a really big city. Big cities are really busy, and can also be very dangerous. So, I think going to school in a smaller city would be much more favorable. Usually the area that surrounds universities in smaller cities is very safe. Also, in small cities the university is usually the focal point, so the community also supports the university a lot. When I go to university, I want to live in a smaller city.

Sample response 2

W: I think the location of a university is important, so I want to go to university in a big city. I think that big cities are much better equipped to help me than small ones. Big cities have more things to see and do, such as museums and concerts. Likewise, the universities in big cities are usually more prominent, so you are more likely to meet important people there. I absolutely want to go to university in a big city.

Transcript

Integrated

Page 105

C

W: The announcement says that a new games room will be built in the dormitory. It will have many activities and will build a strong community. I think the conversation will be about the benefits of the new games room.

Page 106

B

W: Have you seen this notice yet?

M: Yes, I think it's great. I think a games room will really improve life in our dorm. I can't wait for it to be finished.

W: Really? I don't understand the justification for spending our money on a games room. We should be studying at university, not playing around.

M: Well, of course studying is important. But so is relaxing. Sometimes, I need a break from academics to help me focus. Usually, I go somewhere else, but this will be better.

W: Why?

M: Because I won't waste my time going other places. If I need a study break I can come downstairs and play a game of pool. Then I can go back to studying feeling refreshed. Also, I will be able to spend my free time with other students. Even if my friends are busy, I can go to the games room and meet new people. The people occupying the games room will be some of my classmates. I might make new friends or find people I can study with. Hence, I think this will be beneficial for me as a person and a student.

W: I guess you've got some good points. It does sound like fun.

Page 107

D

M: The man thinks this is a good idea. He won't have to travel somewhere else to relax. He can take a break and go back to studying in his room. He might meet new friends or classmates to study with. He thinks it will be beneficial.

Page 108

Step 2

W: I can't believe this announcement.

M: What is it about?

W: The dorm council is planning to renovate the dorm lounge.

M: What are they planning?

W: They're adding an entertainment unit and buying a new TV and DVD player.

M: Don't you think that will be beneficial to residents?

W: Absolutely not. There is no possible justification for this. The dorm lounge is a space for students to interact and study. It is not meant for people to watch movies.

M: Really? I would think that a TV would make more students go to the lounge and relax.

W: That's not really interacting. You can't meet new people and talk when there is a TV on. You can only watch quietly.

M: What do students do there now?

W: Well, I study there all the time. It's usually a nice quiet place to go and find other students who want to study. It's great because I don't have to study alone in my room. Sometimes we can help each other with our assignments. I don't want a TV in the lounge.

M: Maybe you should make your opposition known to the dorm advisor. You could write a letter to the dorm council.

W: That's a great idea. I think I'll do that.

[Unit 10]

Page 111

C

W: My favorite art to look at are paintings because they have so many beautiful colors. My favorite art to make are sculptures because I usually get really dirty. The closest art museum to my home is twenty minutes away.

Page 113

F

Sample response 1

W: Cities should not spend their money on art and art museums. I think that this is a waste of money. Art does not have a direct effect on people's lives whereas good roads, schools, and public transportation help everyone. Public money should go to things that have the most societal benefits. Art is nice, but it is only useful to a few people. Public money should be used on much more important things than art.

Sample response 2

M: I think cities should spend money on art. Art is a great way for people to be proud of their city and it can enrich people's lives. My city has a grand art museum and temporary outdoor art shows and sculptures that help tourism. So, art can even help make money for cities! I think cities should spend public money on things that make people's lives more enjoyable and that help the city. Art is a great way to do both.

Integrated

Page 115

C

M: The passage was about the US armed forces. The US military was first formed in 1775. The US armed forces are run by the president of the US. I think that the lecture will be about the history of the US military.

Page 116

B

W: The US armed forces are seen as the most powerful military in the world. They are over 200 years old. To join them is voluntary. People will only join them if they want to. Women still cannot serve in some combat positions today. The US spends more money on its armed forces than the rest of the world put together. It is made up of the army, the marine corps, the navy, the air force, and the coast guard. They can move quickly and they can be found all over the world. They were first formed to fight in the War of Independence. Years later, they took part in the Civil War. After these wars, the forces became smaller again. Then they grew larger again in the early twentieth century. They played a big part in the Allied force's wins in World Wars I and II. They have been active ever since. They have taken part in conflicts overseas and back in the US. The head of the US armed forces is the US president. He has the final say in what the military does. The heads of the different parts of the forces help him make decisions.

Page 117

D

M: The lecture and the passage were about the history of the US armed forces. The US armed forces were first formed in 1775. They were formed in order to be able to fight the British in the War of Independence. Years later, they fought again in the Civil War. In the early twentieth century the US armed forces grew larger again. They played a large part in helping the Allied forces win World Wars I and II. Today, the US armed forces have around 1.5 million members. The US spends more money on its military than the rest of the world put together. The US armed forces are run by the president of the US.

Page 118

Step 2

M: The US Coast Guard was first formed in 1790. This was when its ships protected the US coast in times like that of the Civil War. This was the first time that it was involved in combat. It is the oldest sea-going service in the US. The modern coast guard was formed in 1915. It was set up as a military service and a branch of the armed forces. Its main jobs are to protect the public, the environment, and US security interests. It can do this overseas and in the US. It is as much a life-saving service as it is an armed force. It has been involved in every big US conflict. It helped to land Allied troops on D-Day in World War II. This was the last time it was made part of the US Navy. Today, it is still a part of the US war in Iraq. One of its main jobs now is port, water-way, and coastal security. Joining it is voluntary, just like with the other armed forces in the US. They have around 41,000 members today. It answers to the US Department of Homeland Security.

[Unit 11]

Independent

Page 121

C

W: The name of my group is the National Honor Society. We volunteer and help people who are not as lucky as we are. I continue to be a part of the group because I know that we are helping people to have better lives.

Page 123

F

Sample response 1

M: I think that it is better to be a regular member of a group. Regular members of a group rarely have a lot of responsibility. If something goes wrong, regular members do not get penalized as much as the leaders. Leaders often also have to deal with a lot more controversy. In addition, being a regular member lets you choose when you want to be enthusiastic about projects. The leader always has to be enthusiastic. This can be extremely tiring.

Sample response 2

W: It is always better to be the leader of a group. Leaders instruct others on what to do, so if there are problems with a project the leader can decide whether to continue or cancel it. Regular members do not have that power. Leaders also have more incentive to work hard because they receive more praise if the project is done well. Finally, it is great to be the leader because people never dismiss your ideas. Everyone listens to the leader!

Integrated

Page 125

B

W: John, how are you?
M: I'm stressed.
W: Why?
M: I have so much work to do and I don't have time to do everything.
W: What do you need to do?
M: This week I have a sociology paper to write, two journal articles to read, and a physics test to prepare for. Also, my boss gave me double shifts this week at the restaurant, so I have no free time.
W: Maybe you should quit your job.
M: That's one option, but this job is really important to me. If I don't have a job, I can't pay my rent or tuition.

C

W: The students are discussing how much work the man has to do this week. He has a lot of school work and he has to go to his job. I think the rest of the conversation will be about how the man can balance his schedule. I think the man should keep his job.

Page 126

A

W: John, how are you?

M: I'm stressed.

W: Why?

M: I have so much work to do and I don't have time to do everything.

W: What do you need to do?

M: This week, I have a sociology paper to write, two journal articles to read, and a physics test to prepare for. Also, my boss gave me double shifts this week at the restaurant, so I have no free time.

W: Maybe you should quit your job.

M: That's one option, but this job is really important to me. If I don't have a job, I can't pay my rent or tuition.

W: Couldn't you get a loan to pay for your expenses?

M: I could, but I can't imagine the accumulation of debt after a year of university. I'd like to finish school without loans to pay back.

W: Student loans are like an investment in your future. After university, you will be able to get a good job and earn a lot of money. So, what are you going to do?

M: I'll probably skip a few classes this week to get caught up. It won't be a big problem.

W: OK. Just read your class syllabus carefully in case there is an attendance requirement in your class.

Page 127

D

M: This conversation is about the man's busy schedule. He is very busy this week at school and at work. The woman thinks that he should quit his job and focus on his school work because that is more important. She says that university is an investment. He needs a good education to get a good job and make money in the future. The man isn't sure. He thinks that he should skip some classes to finish all his assignments. Then he can keep his job and finish school without a debt. I think he should quit his job. A job at a restaurant is not as important as school. Maybe he could borrow money from his parents to pay his tuition.

Page 128

Step 1

W: Hi, Mark. I'm glad you could meet me. I was hoping that you could give me some advice. I know that your major is finance. Since mine is sociology, maybe you can help me with a money problem.

M: I'll do my best. What do you need?

W: Well, I've recently been given some more shifts at work, so I have some extra money. I've been keeping it in the bank, but I read in a journal that young people should invest their money. What do you think?

M: Well, there are both advantages and disadvantages to investments. It's a really good way to save money because it's not in your account. Also, you can earn more money over time. It's usually more than the accumulation of interest in your bank account.

W: Yes, but can I access it if I need the money immediately?

M: Some investments don't allow you to take out your money early. They will charge a fee for that.

W: Oh, that's not good.

M: Also, you could lose money if you choose a risky investment.

W: I never thought of that. My dad says investing will make me more responsible with my money. I guess I'll have to think about it. Thanks.

[Unit 12]

Independent

Page 131

C

W: I bought a new computer. It made me feel bad because I didn't need to get a new computer. I did this because my friend was talking about how great his new computer was.

F

Sample response 1

W: TV is the most influential in determining my actions. The biggest reason is that I watch TV a lot. There is always someone on TV telling me what to do, say, buy, wear, etc., so it is very difficult to resist. TV sometimes overwhelms me because it gives so much information. Eventually, I give in to what the people on TV want me to do because I hear it so often. That is why I think TV is the most influential.

Sample response 2

M: The people around me are the most influential in determining my actions. I often act in the same way as my family and friends. I speak and use similar vocabulary, listen to the same music, etc. as my friends. This is attributed to the fact that I like what they do and I want to fit in. I often observe groups of people eating the same thing, or dressing in a certain way so I think many people are influenced by those around them. I certainly am.

Integrated

Page 135

B

M: For many years, we thought only humans used verbal communication. Some scientists didn't think so. They began to study the vervet monkey.

C

M: Scientists thought that only humans could use verbal communication. Scientists who disagreed began to study the vervet monkey. I think the scientists found out that there are many different animals that use verbal communication.

Page 136

A

M: For many years, we thought only humans used verbal communication. Some scientists didn't think so. They began to study the vervet monkey. They found that they also used verbal communication. The vervet mostly lives in Africa. It is the same size as a cat and lives in small groups. These groups stay within a small amount of territory. A vervet is small, so it has many enemies. Also, the jungle is very dangerous. Snakes, eagles, leopards, and other animals often try to eat it. The vervet makes a loud, oral shriek when it sees a dangerous animal. Scientists analyzed these shrieks. They learned what they are for. They are used to caution other vervets. They found that each shriek is different. They each have an apparent meaning. One shriek means there is an eagle. Then the vervet runs to a small bush. Another shriek means there is a jaguar. This makes the vervet run up a tree. It is important for the vervet to understand its friends. An eagle can easily get a vervet in a tree. A jaguar can get it on the ground. It is important to run to the right place. The scientists' final evaluation showed that the vervet has a vocabulary of about ten words. It seems now that humans and vervets both use verbal communication.

Page 137

D

W: This lecture is about the vervet monkey. At first, we thought only humans could use verbal communication. Then scientists found out that the vervet monkey could use it as well. The vervet is small. It has many enemies. It lives in small groups in the jungle. A vervet makes loud, oral shrieks when it sees an enemy. This is to caution other vervets. Each shriek has an apparent meaning. One shriek means it sees an eagle. Another shriek means it sees a jaguar. The vervet must run when it hears a shriek. It must run to the right place to be safe. The vervet has a vocabulary of about ten words. Humans and vervets both seem to use verbal communication.

Page 138

Step 1

W: The vervets' verbal communication is very difficult to understand. It took many years to understand the shrieks. Many people do not hear any apparent difference. They think the shrieks are the same. Even scientists find it hard to hear. Some scientists even thought that vervets did not talk to each other. Scientists used computers to find out for sure. Computers analyzed the shrieks. Their final evaluation showed that the shrieks were different. Next scientists learned the meaning of each shriek. They first learned that the shrieks were to caution their friends. Scientists then put speakers in the vervets' jungle territory. They hid them in bushes and in trees. The scientists then used tapes. They played each shriek in the jungle. They watched to see what the vervets did. They saw the vervets run to a different place. Later they learned the meaning of each shriek. Scientists want to study other monkeys. They want to see if they can talk. This is difficult. Other monkeys live in much larger territories. This makes it hard to study them. Vervets are small, smart, and live close together. This makes it easy to study them. Scientists have learned a lot from vervets.

[Review 2]

Integrated 1

Page 142

Step 2

M: Sign language is a communication tool used by many adults and children who are deaf or hard of hearing. It is a language that is spoken through hand motions and body language instead of words. Sign language dates back to the eighteenth century. It started in Europe. It is used internationally and signs vary depending on the location. An example of this would be a South American country would have signs that a North American country might not have. Sign language is usually offered as a language class at university. However, sometimes there is not enough interest from the student population for it to be offered. Students who find interest in becoming fluent in sign language are often looking to find a career where they can use it. A good career for those wanting to use sign language is to become a translator. Hospitals or other service-oriented jobs are in need of people who can communicate with those who are non-verbal communicators to better serve them. The most common sign in sign language is "I love you." If anyone is interested in learning sign language, libraries or bookstores have great books for beginners.

Integrated 2

Page 144

Step 1

M: Hey, Michelle. What are you working on?
W: College applications. Have you started working on your applications yet?
M: No . . . I am a bit overwhelmed by the application process. In fact, I am not sure I want to go to college.
W: What would you do instead, Fred?
M: I am thinking about joining the armed forces or maybe traveling for a bit.
W: Last week you mentioned you were interested in architecture.
M: I know. I just don't want to regret not having traveled the world while I'm young.
W: You know you can study abroad in college. That would give you a chance to travel and go to school.
M: I haven't thought about that option. I think I am avoiding having to make a decision.
    It is all kind of overwhelming.
W: Yeah, I agree. You should at least fill the applications out.
M: I plan on it. I still have a few weeks before they are due.
W: I think whatever you decide to do you will have the opportunity to travel.
M: I'm sure you're right, Michelle. Hey, good luck on your applications.
W: Thanks, Fred. Let me know what you decide to do.

[Unit 1]

Independent

Page 15

B

1. My favorite movie is _Mary Poppins_.
2. I first saw this movie <u>when I was a young child</u>.
3. I like this movie because <u>it has great music and a happy ending</u>.

Page 16

A

1. The most recent book I read was _The Hobbit_ by J.R. Tolkien.
2. I did not enjoy the book that much. I think that it was very difficult and slow.
3. The book taught me that it is important to be strong and to have good friends.
4. I would recommend this book to people. It teaches us very important lessons even though it is a little boring.

B

Thrilling	Suspenseful
Mysterious	Slow
Difficult to understand	Not my type
Clever	Well-written
A page-turner	Exciting

C

Which?	The movie _Shrek_ taught me a very positive message.
What?	It taught me to <u>be comfortable with who I am</u>.
How?	It showed this message by <u>having beautiful Princess Fiona turn into an ogre at night</u>.
Why?	This message is important because <u>we should be happy with who we are even if there are things that we don't like about ourselves</u>.

D

Inspirational	Thoughtful
Energizing	Exciting
Optimistic	Caring
Helpful/aiding	Friendly

Page 17

F

Sample response 1

Life is Beautiful

What happened
Story about a specific Jewish family in World War II
Had to endure many hardships
Never gave up hope

How it influenced me
Look for beauty in the world
Looking for beauty can give you hope

Conclusion: Try to find beauty in the world every day

Sample response 2

Book about Mozart

What happened
Talks about music he made
It was beautiful and authentic
Changed people's lives

How it influenced me
Learning to play piano
Learning to write music

Conclusion: Want to have a great cultural impact like Mozart

G

1. authentic   2. specific   3. overcome
4. endure   5. accomplished

Page 18

Sample response 1
Step 2

Movie _Rudy_

What happened
Small, slow university student
Wanted to play American football
Overcame hardships and accomplished his dream

How it influenced me
Teaches me I can do anything
I must work hard to accomplish my dreams
Work hard to become a writer

Conclusion: Like Rudy, work hard to accomplish dreams

Step 3

The <u>movie _Rudy_</u> had a very positive influence on my life. It is about <u>a slow, small university student whose dream was to play American football for his university. Everyone said he was too slow and too small to play, but he overcame this eventually and accomplished his dream.</u> It taught me <u>that I can accomplish my dreams if I endure hardships and work hard</u>. I hope <u>to be a writer one day. Just like Rudy, I work hard every day in class to accomplish my dream</u>.

Sample response 2
Step 2

Book *Green Eggs and Ham*

What happened
Boy wants man to eat green eggs and ham

Man doesn't want to try it

Eventually man eats green eggs and ham

How it influenced me
I must be willing to try new things
I might like it

Conclusion: Like the man, I will try new things and hopefully like them.

Step 3

The book *Green Eggs and Ham* had a very positive influence on my life. It is about a boy who tries to get an older man to try green eggs and ham. The boy endures and eventually the old man tries it and likes green eggs and ham. It taught me that I must be willing to try new things because I might like them. I hope that I will always want to try new things.

Integrated

Page 19

B
1. Buses will not stop at the Preston Road bus stop.
2. Students should begin using the Davis Boulevard stop.
3. I think the conversation will be about what students think of the bus routes changing.

Page 20

B

Man	Woman
• The school is closing the Preston Road bus stop • Take the bus to Davis Boulevard • Walk to SaveMart. • The University doesn't have the money to keep the bus route open	• Not happy about the change • Used bus route to shop at SaveMart • It will be more difficult for students to shop at SaveMart • The university should spend less on the football team and more on buses

Page 21

D
The woman is not happy about the bus route change.
A. It is an inconvenience
　1. to take the bus to SaveMart
　2. to have to shop at the more expensive stores near campus

B. The man
　1. doesn't think it is an inconvenience
　2. thinks the university doesn't have money to keep the bus going

F
1. route　　2. no longer　　3. expensive
4. Repairing　　5. inconvenience

Page 22
Step 2

Woman	Man
• Asks if man knows that the city is closing Kirby Road • Will have to leave at least 15 minutes earlier to get to class on time • The road had big holes. They are terrible. • Thinks they did the right thing by closing the area	• Going to make walk to school longer • Thinks the road needs repair but should be able to walk through area

Page 23

Step 4
The man is not happy about the road closure.
A. The man
　1. is going to have to walk farther to school
　2. thinks the road should be repaired but should let students walk in area
B. The woman
　1. will need to leave earlier to get to school on time
　2. thinks the road needs repair
　3. thinks it could be great exercise

Step 5

The man is not happy about the road closure because he is going to have to walk farther to school. He also thinks the road should be repaired but students should be allowed to walk through the area. The woman will need to leave her apartment earlier to get to school on time. She thinks the road needs repair but also thinks it could be great exercise to have to walk to school.

Check-up

Page 24

1. apartment　　2. enough　　3. bus stop
4. bus system　　5. cultural　　6. Jewish
7. hope　　　　8. hardship

Answer Key

[Unit 2]

Independent

Page 25

B

1. My father is a <u>businessman</u>.
2. He works <u>in an office</u>.
3. He has worked there <u>for fifteen years</u>.

Page 26

A

1. The perfect job is to be a famous singer.
2. I don't know anyone who is a famous singer.
3. The best part about the job is that singers get to make lots of people happy.
4. It is the perfect job because I love to sing and I can get paid lots of money.

B

Doctor	Lawyer
Entrepreneur	Businessman
Teacher	Scientist
CEO	Astronaut

C

Who?   <u>My uncle</u> is really happy with his career.
What?   He works as a <u>doctor</u>.
When?   He started working at his job <u>twenty five years ago</u>.
Why?   He loves his job because <u>he gets to help people</u>.

D

Help others	Lets me be creative
Always learn new things	Lots of respect
Feel satisfied	Sufficient time off
Exciting career	Earn a high salary

Page 27

F
Sample response 1

Reason 1
Need money for food and a house
Support
Artists and singers find it hard to pay rent

Reason 2
Need to support family

Support
Doctors and lawyers have enough money to take care of family.
Conclusion: Bankers and doctors can take care of themselves and their family.

Sample response 2

Reason 1
Lets people be more emotional

Support
They are more satisfied

Reason 2
In a boring job they rarely give their best effort
Support
Only go because it is their duty to go to work.
Conclusion: If you must work, do something that makes you happy and do your best.

G

1. satisfied	2. duty	3. ensure
4. creative	5. sufficient	

Page 28

Sample response 1
Step 2

Reason 1
People work hard and need time to relax
Support
Work can be emotional and need to recover

Reason 2
Time off ensures other interests

Support
Other interests help them to be creative at work
Conclusion: Time off is important in choosing a career.

Step 3

The most important thing when choosing a career is <u>having sufficient time off from work. This is important because people work very hard when they are at work and they need enough time to relax. Working can be very emotional, and people need to have enough time to recover. In addition, lots of time off also ensures that workers have other interests and hobbies. These interests can help them to work hard and be more creative at work. Time off is</u> important when choosing a career.

Sample response 2
Step 2

Reason 1
Makes you feel satisfied

Support
At the end of the day, you feel you did something important

Reason 2
Makes you responsible outside of work also
Support
People will learn to trust and count on you
Conclusion: Responsibility is the most important thing when choosing a career.

Step 3

The most important thing when choosing a career is to have a job with a lot of responsibility. This is important because by having a job with a lot of responsibility, people will always feel satisfied with their work at the end of the day. They will feel that they did something important. In addition, having a job with lots of responsibility will ensure that they will be responsible away from work as well. People will learn to trust and count on you. Responsibility is important when choosing a career.

Integrated

Page 29

B

1. One of the most popular styles of design in the 1920s was Art Deco.
2. Many Art Deco buildings were built with stainless steel and glass.
3. I think that the lecture will be about Art Deco architecture.

Page 30

B

Art Deco
- Was a very popular design style
- It can still be seen on buildings today

Art Deco Designers
- Used modern ideas to come up with new ideas
- Were inspired by African art and new technology

The style
- Was all about looking good
- Used many zigzags and jumbled shapes
- Could be found on shoes and cars
- Is still popular today

The Chrysler Building
- Had a spire and sunburst pattern
- Was made using stainless steel and glass

Page 31

D

The lecture and the passage were about architecture and Art Deco.
A. Art Deco was a
   1. popular design style in the 1920s
   2. very modern style that used old and modern ideas for inspiration
B. The style was
   1. about making the inside and outside of buildings look good
   2. used in many other places

C. Art Deco buildings
   1. often had spires and sunburst patterns on them
   2. were made using stainless steel and glass
All of these things can be seen on the Chrysler building.

F
1. worldwide   2. disposal   3. diverse
4. technical   5. interior

Page 32
Step 2

The Empire State Building
- Is one of the best known Art Deco buildings
- Has appeared in many movies
- Looks like it has vertical stripes going down it
- Was built in 1930
- Took sixteen months to build because of the technical advances in building

The Building's Art Deco Style
- Is unlike other Art Deco buildings
- It does not have any curves or sunbursts on it
- The top has a common Art Deco shape
- It is like a pyramid

The Art Deco Movement
- Was influenced by Egyptian architecture
- Mixed old and new ideas to look to the future

Page 33
Step 4

The passage and lecture were about the Empire State building.
A. The Empire State building
   1. is the tallest skyscraper in New York
   2. is one of the most famous Art Deco buildings
B. Was built using limestone and stainless steel
C. Looks like it has vertical stripes going down it
D. Built quickly because of technical advances in building
E. On top it has an Art Deco pyramid shape
F. The style was influenced by Egyptian architecture

Step 5

The passage and lecture were about the Empire State building. It was built in 1930 and it is the tallest skyscraper in New York. It is one of the best-known Art Deco buildings in the world. It was built using limestone and stainless steel. The building looks like it has vertical stripes running down it. It was built in only sixteen months because of technical advances in building. It has an Art Deco pyramid on top of it. Designers used this style because <u>they were influenced by Egyptian architecture</u>.

Check-up

Page 34

1. movement 2. sunburst 3. Stainless Steel
4. curve   5. career   6. Rent
7. salary   8. emotional

[Unit 3]

Independent

Page 35

B

1. Every day I use <u>my cell phone</u>.
2. I use it <u>all the time</u>.
3. It helps me <u>by allowing me to always be in contact with my friends and family</u>.

Page 36

A

1. I would call my invention the Magical Floater.
2. It would help people lift very heavy things.
3. I want to invent this because I don't like it when something is too heavy to move.
4. It will help others because it will let people of all ages move things around easily.

B

Telephone - allows us to talk to others quickly and easily
The wheel - proved to be a better way to move heavy things or go somewhere quickly
Paper - it is versatile and lets us communicate easily
Concrete - it is versatile and lets us build tall, strong buildings
Boats - it allows us to travel on water

C

What?   The computer lets us <u>get information very quickly</u>.
Where? Now, we can use computers <u>almost anywhere in the world</u>.
How?   Computers have changed our lives because <u>we can talk to anyone in the world at any time</u>.
Why?   Computers are important because <u>aspects of our lives depend on being able to talk to others quickly</u>.

D

A quicker way to travel very long distances
A phone that lets me do everything
A machine that can predict the weather better than traditional methods
A medicine that can cure cancer
A superior way to turn wind into electricity

Page 37

F

Sample response 1

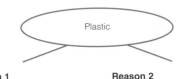

Plastic

Reason 1
Profound effect on how we make everyday things
Support
Lighter, cheaper and easier to shape than wood and metal

Reason 2
Very versatile
Support
Use it in computers, cars, and hospitals

Conclusion: Lives depend on plastic, so it's the greatest invention.

Sample response 2

Airplane

Reason 1
We can go anywhere

Support
Superior to traveling by boat

Reason 2
We can move people and products quickly
Support
Lets us visit far off places and send things quickly

Conclusion: Crucial to our daily lives so the airplane is the greatest invention.

G

1. traditional 2. versatile 3. profound
4. crucial   5. superior

Page 38

Sample response 1

Step 2

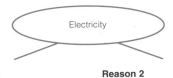

Electricity

Reason 1
It is versatile

Support
Turns on lights, runs phones, keeps us alive in hospitals

Reason 2
Superior to traditional methods of power
Support
Animals and people get tired and need food
Electricity never dies.

Conclusion: Electricity is the greatest invention of them all.

Step 3

Electricity is the greatest invention. It is crucial because it is so versatile. It does everything from turning on lights to running our phones to keeping us alive in hospitals. It also is superior to traditional methods of power. Before, we had to use people or animals when we needed something done. Unlike people and animals, electricity never dies, gets tired, or needs food. Electricity is the greatest invention of them all.

Sample response 2
Step 2

The book

Reason 1
Allowed people to share knowledge
Support
Before books, sharing knowledge depended on talking
This was slow and inefficient

Reason 2
Profound effect on how people learn
Support
Learning became much easier
Let people learn without doing it for themselves.

Conclusion: The book is the greatest invention.

Step 3

The book is the greatest invention. It is crucial because it allowed people to share knowledge and information. Before books, sharing knowledge depended on talking. This was very slow and inefficient. It also had a profound impact on how people learned. Learning became much easier. Books allowed people to learn to do something without actually doing it by themselves first. The book is the greatest invention of them all.

Integrated

Page 39
B
1. The students are discussing the woman's problem.
2. The student saw another student cheating.
3. I think the rest of the conversation will be about what the woman should do.
4. I think the woman should tell her teacher immediately.

Page 40
A

Reasons to tell her professor	Reasons not to tell her professor
• Saw another student cheating • The university's policy is strict • Cheating is wrong • Telling her professor is the right thing to do • He did something bad and should be punished • It's not fair to the other students if someone cheats	• What if he's innocent • Students who cheat are expelled from university • Maybe he's got a good reason for his decision

B
1. The students discuss the fact that cheating is wrong and telling the truth is the right thing to do. Also, it's not fair to the other students if someone cheats.
2. The student shouldn't tell her professor because maybe the student is innocent and he will be expelled for copying. It's also possible that he has a reason for what he did.

Page 41
D
The conversation is about whether the student should tell her teacher what she saw.
A. Reasons for telling her professor
   1. Cheating is wrong
   2. It's not fair to the other students
   3. The student should be punished for cheating
B. Reasons for not telling her professor
   1. Doesn't want to be responsible for the student being expelled
   2. Maybe he had a good reason for what he did
     • Too busy with other school work
     • Personal problems
Conclusion: She should be more understanding of him and check why he did it before she tells a professor.

E
Conclusion: I think the student should tell her professor what she saw because cheating is not a good thing to do and the student who cheated needs to be punished for his actions.

G
1. accuse　　2. Plagiarism　3. policy
4. resort　　5. deceive

Answer Key

Page 42

Test
Step 1

Woman	Man
• Wants to <u>use the man's essay to help her</u> • Won't <u>copy it</u> • Doesn't have <u>any time to do her work</u> • Will give <u>the man one of her essays later</u>	• Is worried about <u>getting into trouble</u> • Doesn't want to <u>be accused of cheating</u> • Needs to <u>think before he makes his decision</u>

Step 3

The conversation is about <u>two students sharing an essay</u>.
A. The woman
   1. wants to <u>borrow the man's essay</u>
   2. doesn't have time to <u>write her essay</u>
   3. will give <u>the man one of her essays</u>
B. The man
   1. is worried about <u>getting in trouble for plagiarism</u>
   2. doesn't want to <u>be accused of cheating</u>
   3. needs to <u>take some time to decide</u>
Conclusion: I would <u>not let the woman use my essay because it is too dangerous and I think it is wrong to cheat</u>.

Page 43

Step 4

The conversation is about <u>sharing an essay</u>. The woman wants to <u>use the man's essay to help her</u> because <u>she doesn't have time to do her own work</u>. She will <u>lend the man one of her essays later</u>. However, the problems with sharing an essay are <u>getting in trouble for plagiarism and being accused of cheating</u>. If I were the man, I would <u>not let the woman use my essay because it is too dangerous and I think it is wrong to cheat</u>.

Check-up

Page 44

1. innocent   2. kick out   3. shame
4. expelled   5. journey   6. depends
7. plastic   8. invention

[Unit 4]

Independent

Page 45

B
1. I respect my <u>cousin Jessie</u>.

2. I respect my <u>cousin</u> because <u>she is kind and diligent and because she always thinks of ways to help other people</u>.
3. I want to be like my <u>cousin</u> because <u>she is loved and respected by so many people</u>.

Page 46

A

1. My friend Scott works to make other people's lives better.
2. He helps collect old jackets to give to poor people.
3. He does this every year in the winter.
4. He helps to make people's lives better by making sure that everyone is warm in the winter.

B

Go to an animal shelter to help neglected animals	Teach a child to read
Collect money for poor people	Help someone who is having a bad day
Spend time with someone who is lonely	Share your wisdom with others
Give money to a charity	Get rid of the garbage in your neighborhood

C

Who?	My favorite athlete is <u>Michael Jordan</u>.
What?	He <u>was a basketball player for the Chicago Bulls</u>.
When?	I started watching him <u>when I was nine years old</u>.
Why?	He is my favorite athlete because <u>he was so good and so exciting to watch</u>.

D

A famous news anchor	The president of your country
Ban Ki-Moon (UN secretary general)	Shaquille O'Neil
George Clooney	A past president of yours or another country

Page 47

F
Sample response 1

Grandfather

Reason 1	**Reason 2**
Overcame a lot	Always gives good advice
Support	**Support**
From poor family	Gave advice whenever I had a
Very diligent	problem
Never neglected his family	Wisdom helped me find an answer to problems

Conclusion: I love and respect my Grandfather so much.

Sample response 2

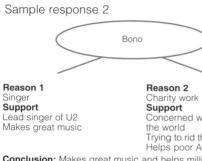

Reason 1
Singer
Support
Lead singer of U2
Makes great music

Reason 2
Charity work
Support
Concerned with people all over the world
Trying to rid the world of poverty
Helps poor African countries

Conclusion: Makes great music and helps millions of people so everyone should respect Bono

G
1. welfare   2. simultaneously   3. charity
4. Diligent   5. neglect

Page 48

Sample response 1
Step 2

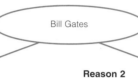

Reason 1
Leads a great charity
Support
Gave forty billion dollars to charity
Gives millions each year to neglected schools, libraries, and students

Reason 2
Looks out for poor Africans
Support
Ensures they have enough to eat
Works to rid Africa of malaria

Conclusion: I think Bill Gates is a great man.

Step 3

   I respect <u>Bill Gates</u> more than anyone else. I respect <u>him</u> because <u>of the charity that he leads. As the world's richest man, he gave over forty billion dollars to his charity. His charity gives millions of dollars every year to neglected schools, libraries, and students</u>. Simultaneously, he <u>looks out for the welfare of poor Africans. He does this by ensuring that they have enough to eat and working to rid Africa of the dangerous disease Malaria</u>. I think <u>Bill Gates</u> is a great man.

Sample response 2
Step 2

Reason 1
Good to everyone
Support
Friends with everyone he meets
Always looks out for their welfare

Reason 2
Makes me feel great
Support
Diligent in sharing wisdom
Makes sure I am doing the right things
Always makes time for me

Conclusion: Thinks older brother is a great man.

Step 3

   I respect <u>my older brother</u> more than anyone else. I respect <u>him</u> because <u>he is so good to everyone. He is friends with everyone that he meets and always looks out for their welfare.</u> Simultaneously, he <u>makes me feel great. He is very diligent in sharing his wisdom with me. He always makes sure that I am doing the right thing and always makes extra time for me.</u> I think <u>my older brother</u> is a great man.

Integrated

Page 49

B
1. It is about <u>a very special plant</u>.
2. It is different because <u>it is a carnivore</u>.
3. I think the plant has to do this because <u>it is really hungry</u>.

Page 50

A
- Special plant
- Different because <u>it is a carnivore</u>
- Called a <u>Venus Flytrap</u>
- They eat <u>insects</u> because <u>their soil is deficient</u>
- Eating insects <u>gives them more nutrients to become big and strong</u>
- Also need <u>air and water to live</u>
- Leaves are <u>round and flat with long fingers at the end</u>
- When an insect stimulates the hairs it <u>snaps shut around the insect</u>
- Plant emits <u>juices</u> to <u>kill the insect and then digests the juices</u>
- Plant must be careful because <u>if the insect is too big it can get sick. If it's too small, it will not get enough food</u>

B
1. The professor says that Venus Flytraps must be carnivores because <u>they have deficient soil. Eating insects gives them more nutrients to become big and strong</u>.
2. The professor says that the Venus Flytrap must be careful because <u>if an insect is too big, the plant can get sick and die. If it is too small, it will not get enough food</u>.

Page 51

D

The lecture is about a <u>carnivore</u> plant named the <u>Venus Flytrap</u>.

A. What it needs to live
1. Insects: <u>gives them more nutrients to be big and strong</u>
   • Needs them because <u>of deficient soil</u>
2. Air and Water: <u>also needed to live</u>
B. Leaves
1. Shape: <u>round and flat with long fingers</u>
2. Each leaf has <u>a series of hairs</u>.
C. When insects touch the leaf it <u>snaps shut around the insect</u>
D. The plant <u>emits juices</u>
1. This <u>kills the insect</u>
2. The plant then <u>digests the juices</u>
E. Must be careful because <u>if it eats something too big or too small, it can die</u>
Conclusion: Venus Flytraps are <u>a very special plant</u>.

F
1. series   2. emits   3. factor
4. deficient   5. stimulate

Page 52
Step 1

• All carnivore plants <u>live in areas with deficient soil, and get a lot of sun and water</u>

• Different plants catch insects in different ways.

• The Venus Flytrap uses a <u>snap trap</u>

• When the leaf is stimulated, <u>it snaps shut</u>

• Another kind of plant catches insects with glue.

• When an insect touches the leaf, <u>it gets stuck, and can't leave</u>

• Lobster Traps are usually found <u>in the sea</u>

• They work because <u>it is easy to go inside the plant, but hard to get out</u>

• Bowl-shaped plants emit <u>juices that insects want to eat</u>

• The walls are high, so <u>the insect can't climb out</u>

Step 3

The lecture is about how carnivore plants catch insects.
A. Snap traps: Leaves snap shut when <u>leaves are stimulated</u>
B. Catches with glue
1. Plants emit <u>glue</u>
2. When insects <u>touch the leaf, they get stuck, and can't leave</u>
C. Lobster Trap
1. Usually found <u>in the sea</u>
2. It's easy <u>to get in</u>
3. It's difficult <u>to get out</u>

D. Bowl-shaped plant
1. Plant emits <u>juices</u>
2. Insects want to <u>eat the juice</u>
3. The insects <u>fall into the bowl and they can't climb out</u>
Conclusion: Many ways <u>carnivore plants catch their food</u>

Page 53
Step 4

   This lecture is about <u>different kinds of carnivore plants</u>. All carnivore plants are the same because <u>they live in areas with deficient soil, but they get a lot of sun and water</u>. But they are different because <u>they catch insects in different ways</u>. The snap trap plants <u>snap shut when the leaf is stimulated</u>. Other plants use glue. When insects touch <u>the leaf, they can't leave</u>. Lobster traps are easy <u>for insects to go in,</u> but <u>difficult for them to get back out of</u>. Bowl plants catch insects by <u>emitting juice that insects want to eat</u>. The insect then <u>falls into the bowl, but it can't climb out.</u>

Check-up

Page 54
1. digest   2. snap   3. carnivores
4. juice   5. wisdom   6. respect
7. rid   8. leading

[Unit 5]

Independent

Page 55
B
1. I recently celebrated <u>Chuseok</u>.
2. For <u>Chuseok</u>, I <u>helped my family make the traditional dish, songpyon</u>.
3. I enjoyed the holiday because <u>I got to see all of my cousins, aunts, and uncles</u>.

Page 56
A
1. My friend celebrates Ramadan.
2. Muslims celebrate Ramadan.
3. During Ramadan, my friend doesn't eat or drink between sunrise and sunset.
4. He celebrates this holiday to honor his religion and to become a better Muslim.

B

New Year's Day Independence Day
Thanksgiving Constitution Day
Christmas Buddha's Birthday
Lunar New Year Memorial Day
Easter

C

What? In my country, <u>Thanksgiving</u> is a national holiday.

When? We celebrate <u>Thanksgiving every year on the third Thursday in November</u>.

Why? We celebrate <u>Thanksgiving</u> because <u>it is a time to be together with all of our family and friends</u>.

What? Every year we <u>have a giant dinner with a big turkey to celebrate Thanksgiving</u>.

D

Go to my grandma's house Go to church
Pray with my family Have a big
Honor my parents and celebration
grandparents Go to a parade
Stay home from school Eat delicious food
Go to the swimming pool Take a vacation

Page 57

F

Sample response 1

Rosh Hashona

What I do
Family gathers for dinner
Go to a ceremony
Listen to stories

Why I like it
Sometimes a great story
Get the day off from school

Conclusion: Favorite part is that I get the day off from school.

Sample response 2

Memorial Day

What I do
Honor people who died fighting wars
Have barbeque parties

Why I like it
Means beginning of summer
Barbeque parties
Summer vacation will start soon

Conclusion: Memorial day means that summer vacation will start in a few weeks.

G

1. ceremonies 2. religion 3. national
4. resist 5. honor

Page 58

Sample response 1
Step 2

New Year's Day

What I do
Gather with all friends
Have a big party

Why I like it
Everyone is in a good mood
Get to have a great time with friends

Conclusion: I love New Year's Day because I can have a great time with all my friends.

Step 3

My favorite holiday is <u>New Year's Day</u>. Every year I <u>gather with my friends from all around the country and we have a giant celebration. We invite all our friends over to our house and we have a big party</u>. It's great because <u>it is a national holiday so everyone is in a good mood</u>. But mostly, I love <u>New Year's Day</u> because <u>I get to have such a great time with all my friends</u>.

Sample response 2
Step 2

Valentine's Day

What I do
Go with my girlfriend to nice restaurant
Say we won't buy gifts, but cannot resist and buy gifts anyway

Why I like it
Spend time with my girlfriend
It's a special day
Remember and talk about the day for the rest of the year

Step 3

My favorite holiday is <u>Valentine's Day</u>. Every year I <u>go with my girlfriend to a nice restaurant. We always tell each other not to buy presents, but we cannot resist and buy presents for each other anyway</u>. It's great because <u>I get to spend a lot of time with my girlfriend</u>. But mostly, I love <u>Valentine's Day</u> because <u>it is a special day that we remember and talk about for the rest of the year</u>.

Integrated

Page 59

B

1. The <u>"Beginning of Term Picnic" is happening on Friday</u>.
2. There will be <u>live music and games with prizes</u>.
3. I think the conversation will be about <u>the students' interest in the picnic</u>.

Answer Key

Page 60

B

Man	Woman
• Thinks the picnic is <u>a terrible idea</u> • Thinks there are better ways to <u>spend the students' tuition</u> • Thinks the university should buy <u>essential things</u> • Knows the library needs <u>new computers</u> • Thinks it's also <u>a waste of time</u> • Thinks students should <u>study</u> not <u>play games</u> • Says his sister <u>went to the picnic last year and didn't like it</u> • Won't <u>go to the picnic</u> • Will write <u>a letter of protest</u>	• Knows there will be <u>food, games, and entertainment</u> • Thinks fun is <u>also important</u> • Thinks the man <u>shouldn't go to the picnic</u>

Page 61

D

The man thinks the picnic is <u>a bad idea</u>.
A. Thinks it is a waste
   1. of <u>the university's money</u>
   2. of <u>the students' time</u>
B. The man says
   1. the university should buy <u>essential things</u>
   2. the library needs <u>new computers</u>
C. He decides that he won't <u>go to the picnic</u>

F

1. voucher   2. protest   3. impose
4. attendance   5. essential

Page 62

Step 2

Woman	Man
• Asks the man for a <u>ride to the campus events office</u> • Wants to go at <u>6 a.m.</u> • Wants to get <u>a ticket for a concert</u> • Tells the man the concert is <u>free</u> • Invites the man to <u>go to the concert</u> • Knows the concert is going to be <u>filmed for a music video</u> • Convinces the man <u>to miss his class and go to the concert</u>	• Thinks the ticket will be <u>expensive</u> • Has <u>a class at the time of the concert</u> • Worries that he might <u>miss something important</u> • Agrees to <u>take the woman to the campus events office and to go to the concert</u>

Page 63

Step 4

The woman is <u>excited about the free concert</u>.
A. The woman
   1. needs to go to <u>the campus events office at 6 a.m.</u>
   2. wants to pick up <u>a ticket for a concert</u>

B. She thinks the concert will be good because
   1. the tickets are <u>free</u>
   2. the concert will be <u>filmed for a music video</u>

Step 5

The woman is <u>excited about the free concert</u>. She needs to go to <u>the campus events office at 6 a.m.</u> to <u>pick up a ticket for the concert.</u> She thinks the concert will be good because <u>the tickets are free</u> and because <u>the concert will be filmed for a music video</u>.

Check-up

Page 64

1. gymnasium   2. honestly
3. picnic   4. held
5. pray   6. war
7. holidays   8. celebration

[Unit 6]

Independent

Page 65

B
1. I live in <u>Taipei</u>.
2. My city is famous for <u>our beautiful building, Taipei 101</u>.
3. People should visit my city because <u>they can eat all the great food and go to the top of one of the tallest buildings in the world</u>.

Page 66

A

1. Recently, I visited Chicago.
2. I visited Chicago to see my aunt and uncle.
3. While in Chicago, I went to a baseball game and I went to the top of the Sears Tower.
4. I want to go back to Chicago because I had so much fun at the baseball game, so I want to do that again.

B

Friendly people	Tasty food
Things to do	Ability of people to speak
Architecture	English well
Fashion styles	Colorful scenery
	Good shopping

C

How?   The buildings in my city would <u>be built with material that has been recycled, to help the environment</u>.

Where?	I would build my city <u>in a place that has great weather that is somewhere between mountains and the sea</u>.
What?	My city would have <u>great public transportation and everyone would be fluent in two languages</u>.
Why?	My city would be special because <u>of the beautiful scenery and the friendliness of the people</u>.

D

Great Wall of China - Beijing
Eiffel Tower - Paris

St. Basil's Cathedral - Moscow
Statue of Liberty - New York

Long, white sandy beaches - Rio de Janeiro
Imperial Palace - Kyoto

Page 67

F

Sample response 1

Sydney

Reason 1
Nice and clean
Support
Has beautiful architecture
Opera House and Harbor
Bridge
Great beaches
Can surf

Reason 2
Everyone is fluent in English
Support
Can communicate easily

Conclusion: One day I would like to immigrate to Sydney.

Sample response 2

Istanbul

Reason 1
Has so much history
Support
Buildings are really old and beautiful

Reason 2
Great feeling to the city
Support
Informal but has lots of energy
People are friendly and willing to help
Great food

Conclusion: I love Istanbul.

G

1. informal
2. immigrate
3. architecture
4. fluent
5. reside

Page 68

Sample response 1
Step 2

Yangshou, China

Reason 1
Incredible Scenery
Support
Big green hills that come from nowhere
Architecture of the city fits scenery well

Reason 2
Has a great feeling
Support
Informal and laid back
Friendly and helpful people live there

Conclusion: Yangshou is the best city.

Step 3

The best city that I have visited is <u>Yangshou in China</u>. It is amazing because <u>of the incredible scenery there. The whole city has these really big green hills that just come from nowhere. The architecture of the city also fits the scenery very well. In addition, Yangshou has a great feeling to it. It is really informal and laid back. All the people who reside there are really friendly and are always willing to help you. Yangshou</u> is the best city.

Sample response 2
Step 2

Budapest

Reason 1
Really beautiful architecture
Support
Has beautiful green and gold roofs
Buildings look perfect next to each other

Reason 2
Informal city
Support
Perhaps because aren't many tourists there
Can enjoy the city without being in a hurry

Conclusion: Budapest is the best city.

Step 3

The best city that I have visited is <u>Budapest</u>. It is amazing because <u>it has really beautiful architecture. All the roofs in the old town have beautiful green and gold colors. Each building looks perfect beside the building next to it. In addition, Budapest is a very informal city. Perhaps this is because there don't seem to be many tourists there. This lets you enjoy the city without being in a hurry. Budapest</u> is the best city.

Answer Key

Page 69

B

1. Geology is the science of the <u>solid matter</u> that makes up the Earth. It looks at <u>rocks and soils</u>.
2. When molten rock reaches the Earth's surface, it <u>explodes through the ground</u>.
3. I think that the lecture will be about <u>volcanoes</u>.

Page 70

B

Volcanoes
- An opening in the Earth's surface that <u>lets out molten rock, ash, and gases</u>
- The explosions can be <u>hazardous to all life nearby</u>
- They can be found <u>on the seabed and on land, too</u>

Mountains
- The explosions can cause <u>mountains to appear over time</u>
- This is because the molten rock <u>cools and becomes hard on the surface</u>

Causes
- Volcanoes can be caused by the movement of <u>plates on the Earth's surface</u>
- They can also occur where <u>the Earth's crust is thin</u>
- These places are called <u>hotspots</u>

Terms
- Volcanoes are called active when <u>they erupt often</u>
- They are called dormant when <u>they are not erupting</u>
- They are called extinct when <u>they are not expected to erupt again</u>

Page 71

D

The lecture and the passage were about <u>volcanoes and where they can occur</u>.
A. Volcanoes
   1. occur when <u>molten rock, ash, and gases escape from beneath the Earth's crust</u>
   2. are full of molten rock <u>called magma</u>
   3. erupt with <u>a big explosion</u>
B. Volcanic eruptions
   1. can happen <u>on the seabed or on land</u>
   2. can cause <u>mountains to form as the magma cools down</u>
C. Volcanoes appear
   1. when <u>plates of land on the Earth's surface move</u>
   2. in places <u>where the Earth's crust is very thin</u>
D. Volcanoes have different <u>names depending on how regularly they erupt</u>

F

1. climactic   2. hazardous   3. repeatedly
4. explode   5. Matter

Page 72

Step 2

Hotspots
- One of the best known is <u>under Yellowstone park in the US</u>

Yellowstone Park
- It has several craters called <u>calderas</u>
- The Yellowstone Caldera is <u>called a supervolcano</u>

Supervolcanoes
- When they erupt <u>they can change the land around them</u>
- They can <u>affect the weather all over the world</u>

Yellowstone Caldera
- Has not erupted <u>in over half a million years</u>
- Under it is <u>a large body of magma</u>
- It is covered in <u>hot water and steam</u>

Geysers
- Are where hot water and <u>steam shoot up through the ground</u>
- There are <u>over 300 of them in the park</u>

Page 73

Step 4

The lecture and the passage were about <u>Yellowstone Park</u>.
A. Yellowstone Park
   1. Is said to be on <u>top of a hotspot</u>
   2. Has several <u>craters</u>
B. Yellowstone Caldera is <u>an active supervolcano</u>
C. Old lava covers <u>most of the park</u>
D. Under the park <u>is a large body of magma</u>
   1. This is covered <u>in hot water and steam</u>
   2. It can escape <u>up through the ground in geysers</u>
   3. This steam also heats <u>thousands of hot springs and mud pools</u>

Step 5

The passage and the lecture were about <u>Yellowstone Park</u>. Underneath Yellowstone Park is one of the best known <u>hotspots in the world</u>. The park has <u>several craters in it</u>. One of them, called Yellowstone Caldera, is an <u>active supervolcano</u>. In the park, old lava <u>covers most of the land</u>. Underneath the park is <u>a large body of magma,</u> which is covered in <u>hot water and steam</u>. This can escape <u>up through the ground, where boiling water and steam shoot up into the air</u>. This steam and magma also heat <u>thousands of hot springs and mud pools</u>.

Page 74

1. seabed
2. hotspot
3. dormant
4. molten
5. opera
6. surf
7. scenery
8. Perhaps

[Review 1]

Independent 1

Page 75

Sample response 1

Step 2

Movies with happy endings

Movies with happy endings   **Movies with sad endings**
Why:
Light hearted
Why not:
Don't make you think as much   Don't laugh as much
Better because: Movies with happy endings are going to be more light-hearted and filled with laughter.

Step 3

   When I watch a movies, I prefer to <u>watch ones with happy endings</u>. I like <u>happy endings because they make me laugh and they tend to be more light hearted</u>. I prefer not to watch <u>movies that have sad endings</u> because they <u>make me think a lot more and I don't laugh as much</u>. I enjoy being able to watch movies <u>and not have to think too much</u>.

Sample response 2

Step 2

Movies with sad endings

Movies with happy endings   **Movies with sad endings**
Why:
                           More meaning to movie
Why not:
Don't make you think as much   Don't laugh as much
Better because: Movies with sad endings tend to have more meaning.

Step 3

   When I watch movies, I prefer to <u>watch ones with sad endings</u>. I like <u>sad endings because they make me think more and the movie tends to have more meaning</u>. I prefer not to watch <u>movies that have happy endings</u> because they <u>don't make me think as much</u>. I enjoy being able to watch movies <u>that have meaning</u>.

Page 76

Step 2

Man	Woman
• Asks if attending <u>graduation ball</u> • Asks why woman needs <u>permission</u> to go • Going to school in summer is better than <u>going to school in the fall</u> • If not going to ball <u>come hangout</u>	• Not sure if attending. Depends on if <u>administration gives permission</u> • Should know by <u>end of week</u> • Missing credits in <u>technical writing and math</u> • The graduation ball is only for <u>graduating students</u>

Page 77

Step 4

The conversation is about <u>the administration's choice in letting the woman attend the graduation ball</u>.
A. The woman might not <u>be able to attend the graduation ball</u>
B. She is waiting
  1. on <u>the administration to make a decision</u>
  2. to see whether <u>she can attend the ball</u>
C. The man thinks
  1. it is <u>a huge inconvenience</u>
  2. it would be <u>better if she graduated in the summer</u> rather then <u>in the fall</u>

Step 5

   The woman expresses that there is a chance she will not <u>be able to attend the graduation ball</u> because <u>she might not be able to graduate this spring</u>. She is waiting <u>on the administration to make a decision</u> whether <u>she can attend the ball</u>. She now needs to decide between <u>taking classes in the summer or the fall</u>. The man thinks it is <u>a huge inconvenience</u> but thinks <u>taking classes in the summer is better than in the fall</u>.

Page 78

Step 1

- Botany is the study of plants
- There are <u>several different</u> ways to <u>categorize plants</u>
- Annuals, <u>perennials</u>, and <u>biennials</u> are three categories that <u>describe a plant's life span</u>
- Trees and shrubs are usually <u>perennials</u>
- Biennials produce leaves in the first year and <u>in the second produce flowers and seeds</u>
- Annuals are less likely to <u>survive cold weather</u>

Answer Key

Step 3

The lecture is about botany and the life span of plants.
A. Annuals
    1. live for <u>up to one year</u>
    2. are <u>less likely to survive cold weather</u>
B. Perennials
    1. live <u>more than two years</u>
    2. are <u>more likely to endure the cold weather</u>
C. Biennials
    1. live <u>up to two years</u>
    2. are <u>more likely to endure the cold weather</u>
Conclusion: Perennials and biennials are more likely to survive in the cold weather.

Page 79

Step 4

The lecture is about botany and the life span of plants. Plants can be categorized by their life span in three categories: <u>annuals, perennials, and biennials</u>. Annuals live <u>up to one year</u>. Perennials live <u>more than two years</u> and biennials live <u>up to two years</u>. Annuals are the <u>least likely to survive in cold weather</u>. Perennials and biennials are <u>more likely to endure cold weather</u> because they fall dormant in the wintertime.

Independent 2

Page 80

Sample response 1
Step 2

School Activities
Good reasons:
Get to play with friends from school
Don't have to leave school
Bad reasons:
I prefer: school activities because I get to be with my friends and I don't have to leave school

Activities away from school
No friends

Step 3

    I prefer to do <u>school activities</u>. My favorite <u>school activity is playing soccer</u>. I get to <u>play with my friends from school</u>. I also like that I get to <u>be with my friends and I don't have to leave school. I don't have many friends outside of school, and I don't need any because I have so many at school</u>.

Sample response 2
Step 2

<svg>Activities away from school</svg>

School Activities
Good reasons:

Activities away from school
Meet new people
Go into the city

Bad reasons:
Stay at school

I prefer: activities away from school because I get to meet new people and go into the city

Step 3

    I prefer to do <u>activities away from school</u>. My favorite <u>activity to do away from school is taking guitar lessons</u>. I get to <u>take lessons with four other students from different schools at a music store in the city</u>. I also like that I get to <u>meet different people and that I get to do something away from school</u>.

[Unit 7]

Independent

Page 81

B
1. I last traveled to <u>Paris</u>.
2. I went with <u>my friends Dave and Dan</u>.
3. My vacation could have been better if <u>I were able to speak French</u>.

Page 82

A
1. The best thing about traveling alone is that I can do exactly what I want to do.
2. The worst thing about traveling alone is that I don't have people who can help me when I get into trouble.
3. The best thing about traveling with a tour is that I don't have to worry about anything.
4. The worst thing about traveling with a tour is that I might be in a group with people who I don't like.

B
Lose your luggage
Have money stolen

Miss your flight
Get lost

Be homesick and miss your family
Get sick from food

Run out of money
Be tired from flying

C

Where?	I would go to <u>Egypt</u>.
Who?	I would go with <u>my family on a tour</u>.
Why?	I would go with <u>my family on a tour</u> because <u>I would be worried that I would get lost</u>.
What?	I would want to see <u>the Great Pyramids and the Sphinx</u>.

D

Go shopping for souvenirs

Go to the beach

Look at the sites

Meet new people

Eat food

Stay in nice hotels

Go out at night

Act on my impulses

Page 83

F

Sample response 1

Traveling alone is better

Reason 1
Can take whichever route you want
Support
Can act on all your impulses

Reason 2
In a group you must stay with the group
Support
Can be boring and a waste of time
Stop at souvenir stands

Conclusion: Don't like shopping so prefer to travel alone.

Sample response 2

Traveling in a group is better

Reason 1
Never lonely
Support
Always someone to talk to

Reason 2
Ensures you will see everything
Support
Tour guide can decide how much time to spend at each site

Conclusion: Traveling in a group can be cheaper.

G

1. investigate　　2. guide　　3. tours
4. impulses　　5. appropriate

Page 84

Sample response 1

Step 2

Mix of tours and traveling by yourself

Reason 1
Lets you decide what is appropriate for you
Support
Can decide what you really want to see and do

Reason 2
Investigate a small tour to ensure you will see everything
Support
Makes sure you get good information

Conclusion: The best way to travel is a mix of tours and independent travel.

Step 3

When traveling, I think it's better to <u>go using a mix of traveling by yourself and going with a group</u>. Going <u>by yourself lets you decide what things are most appropriate for you. You can then decide what you really want to see and do rather than just joining a group immediately</u>. Once you decide <u>what you want to do, it's a great idea to investigate and join a small tour. This will ensure that you see everything and get good information</u>. The best way to travel is <u>with a mix of tours and independent travel</u>.

Sample response 2
Step 2

Traveling with a group of friends

Reason 1
Can act on impulses
Support
Know each other and can do what you want

Reason 2
Can be cheaper
Support
Share costs of hotels and car rentals

Conclusion: Traveling with a small group is best because you can choose a route without being lonely.

Step 3

When traveling, I think it's better to <u>go with a group of four friends, but not on a tour</u>. Going <u>with friends ensures that you can act on impulse. With my friends, we all like the same things, so deciding what to do is easy, but if you join a tour you will have to do things you don't want to do</u>. Once you decide <u>remember that going with a small group can also be cheaper because you share the costs of things like hotels and car rentals</u>. The best way to travel is <u>with a group of friends because you can choose your own route without being lonely</u>.

Integrated

Page 85

B

1. The students are discussing <u>the woman's schedule</u>.
2. The woman has <u>basketball practice and a class at the same time</u>.
3. I think the rest of the conversation will be about <u>whether the woman should take the class or go to basketball practice</u>.
4. I think the woman should choose <u>the class</u>.

Answer Key

A

Reasons for taking a class	Reasons for going to practice
• Professor is <u>famous and the syllabus looks great</u> • Would learn <u>a lot</u> • Student needs <u>a science course</u> • Loved <u>her last anthropology course</u>	• Basketball is <u>her passion</u> • Been playing <u>for a very long time</u> • Wants to <u>be on the national team</u> • Came to school <u>on a basketball scholarship</u>

B
1. The students discuss <u>the famous teacher and the great syllabus. Also, the student needs to take a science course and she likes anthropology</u>.
2. The student should go to practice because <u>basketball is her passion and she has been playing for a long time. Also, she needs to practice to be on the national team and keep her basketball scholarship</u>.

Page 87
D
The conversation is about <u>the woman's schedule</u>.
A. Should take the course because
   1. the teacher is <u>very famous</u>
   2. the student needs <u>science credits</u>
   3. she really <u>likes anthropology</u>
B. Should go to basketball practice because
   1. it is her <u>passion</u>
   2. she has been <u>playing for a long time</u>
   3. she has to <u>practice to get on the national team</u>
   4. she has a <u>scholarship</u>
Conclusion: I think <u>she should quit basketball</u> because <u>school is more important</u>.

E
Conclusion: I think <u>she should quit basketball</u> because <u>she needs science credits and likes anthropology</u>.

G
1. coach   2. absence   3. passion
4. qualify   5. Anthropology

Page 88
Step 1

Woman	Man
• Wants the man to <u>come to her birthday party</u> • Her birthday is <u>tomorrow night</u> • Thinks there must be <u>another coach for the team</u> • Other friends will <u>be very upset</u>	• Has <u>other plans</u> • Is the <u>assistant coach</u> of his <u>brother's soccer team</u> • Tomorrow is <u>an important game</u> • Knows his brother will <u>notice if he's not there</u> • Should keep <u>his promise</u>

Step 3
The conversation is about <u>the man's plans for tomorrow</u>.
A. The woman
   1. wants the man to <u>come to her party</u> because <u>it's only once a year</u>
   2. thinks there must be <u>another coach for the team</u>
   3. knows their friends will <u>be upset if he doesn't come</u>
B. The man
   1. is the <u>assistant coach of his brother's soccer team</u>
   2. knows tomorrow is <u>a very important game</u>
   3. knows his brother <u>will be upset if he misses the game</u>
   4. wants to <u>keep his promise</u>
Conclusion: I think <u>he should go to the soccer game.</u>

Page 89
Step 4

The conversation is about <u>the man's plans for tomorrow</u>. The woman wants the man to <u>come to her party</u> because <u>it's only once a year</u>. She thinks that there <u>must be another coach for the team</u>, so <u>no one will miss him</u>. Also, their friends will be <u>disappointed if they don't see him</u>. The man has to <u>coach his brother's soccer team</u> because tomorrow <u>is a very important game</u>. His brother <u>will know</u> if <u>he misses it</u> and he wants to <u>keep his promise</u>.

I think the man should <u>keep his promise to his brother and go to the game</u> because <u>it will make his brother really happy</u>.

I think the man should <u>go to his friend's birthday</u> because <u>he can go to the soccer games anytime</u>.

Check-up
Page 90
1. quit   2. homesick   3. syllabus
4. frustrated   5. lonely   6. souvenirs
7. quarter   8. act

[Unit 8]

Independent

Page 91
B
1. I normally start studying for a test <u>a week before the exam</u>.
2. I prepare for my test by <u>reading over my class notes and underlining the important areas</u>.
3. I normally feel <u>excited</u> before taking a test.

Page 92

A

1. A good thing about studying at home for a test is that it is always quiet.
2. A bad thing about studying at home for a test is that it is difficult to have my questions answered.
3. A good thing about studying at school for a test is that my friends are there to help me when I have problems.
4. A bad thing about studying at school for a test is that I stay at school really late, and so I go to bed late.

B

Reread my notes	Rewrite my notes
Study with a friend	Do extra practice problems
Talk with my teacher	Visit my tutor
Review the curriculum	Answer all the things that I find unclear

C

What?	I studied for my <u>science</u> test.
Where?	For my <u>science</u> test, I studied at <u>home</u>.
How long?	I studied for <u>three hours for the test</u>.
How?	I did <u>really well</u> on my test.

D

Nervous	Scared
Confused	Confident
Excited	Happy
Relieved	Eager
Ecstatic	Worried

Page 93

F

Sample response 1

Reason 1
Keen to go home

Reason 2
If I stay at school, friends will distract me

Support
Never want to extend time at school

Conclusion: Home is quiet with nothing to do, so I can focus much more on studies.

Sample response 2

Reason 1
Something will be unclear
Support
Can ask classmates

Reason 2
All books are at school
Support
Helps to answer questions that are needed before the test

Conclusion: Even though I have to stay late, I never regret studying at school.

G

1. anticipate   2. regret   3. curriculum
4. inevitably   5. extend

Page 94

Sample response 1
Step 2

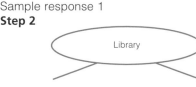

Reason 1
Always quiet

Reason 2
Can find books for curriculum at the library

Support
No one to distract me

Support
Other students use important books at school
Library copies are rarely in use

Conclusion: Studying at the library is the best.

Step 3

The best place for me to study is <u>neither at home nor at school but at the library</u>. I am always keen to study at <u>the library</u> because <u>it is always quiet. People never distract me</u>. More importantly, <u>I can also find all the things I need for my curriculum at the library. At school, other students are inevitably using the important books. At the library, though, no other students are there so I can use the books I need</u>. Studying at the <u>library</u> is the best.

Sample response 2
Step 2

Reason 1
Has everything I need
Support
Other students can help explain things
Books and Internet is available

Reason 2
Has coffee
Support
Need coffee to help me to study

Conclusion: Studying at the coffee shop is the best.

Step 3

The best place for me to study is <u>neither at home nor at school but at a coffee shop</u>. I am always keen to study at <u>the coffee shop</u> because <u>it has everything I need. There are other students who can help me understand things that are unclear. I also have other books and the Internet is available</u>. More importantly, <u>the coffee shop has coffee. I always anticipate that I will need some coffee to help me study</u>. Studying at the <u>coffee shop</u> is the best.

Answer Key

Page 95

B

1. The lecture is mainly about <u>Sherlock Holmes</u>.
2. The authors all <u>created characters that are still remembered</u>.
3. I think the professor will discuss <u>why Sherlock Holmes is so famous</u>.

Page 96

A

- Sherlock Holmes was created <u>by Arthur Conan Doyle</u>.
- Holmes was a <u>detective who lived in London. He was a brilliant man</u>.
- He was able to <u>analyze vague clues very well and predict what happened</u>.
- The last explanation <u>would usually implicate someone</u>.
- His friend, <u>Dr. Watson, helped him find clues</u>.
- His enemy, <u>Professor Moriarty, often did bad things</u>.
- Holmes often <u>smoked a pipe and wore a strange hat</u>.
- People still <u>read and meet together to talk about Sherlock Holmes</u>.

B

1. He was able to predict what happened because <u>he was able to analyze vague clues well</u>.
2. Sherlock Holmes often wore <u>a strange hat and often smoked pipes</u>.

Page 97

D

The lecture is about <u>Sherlock Holmes</u>.
A. Analyzing clues
  1. Holmes analyzed clues <u>very well</u>
  2. He was usually <u>correct</u>
  3. The last explanation usually <u>implicated someone</u>
B. About Holmes
  1. Friend: <u>Dr. Watson</u>
  2. Enemy: <u>Professor Moriarty</u>
  3. Clothes and Habits: <u>wore a strange hat, smoked a pipe</u>
Conclusion: People still <u>read and talk about Sherlock Holmes</u>.

F

1. predict   2. schemes   3. analyze
4. vague   5. implicated

Page 98

Step 1

- Arthur Conan Doyle led a very interesting life.
- He was born in <u>Edinburgh, Scotland</u>.
- He went to university <u>to become a doctor</u>.
- He wrote <u>his first Sherlock Holmes story in 1882</u>.
- It was called <u>*A Study in Scarlet*</u>.
- He used his fame <u>to help others</u>.
- He helped people who <u>were wrongly implicated of crimes</u>.
- He ran for <u>parliament two times but lost</u>.
- Idea of Holmes is <u>vague</u>
- May have come from one of his <u>professors</u>
- May have come from Edgar Allen Poe's <u>character C. Auguste Dupin</u>
- Holmes and Doyle were equally brilliant men.

Step 3

The lecture is about Arthur Conan Doyle's interesting life.
A. His life
  1. Was born in <u>Edinburgh, Scotland</u>
  2. Went to University to be a <u>doctor</u>
  3. Wrote first story in <u>1882</u>
    - It was called <u>*A Study in Scarlet*</u>
    - It was very <u>popular</u>
  4. He helped others
    - He helped people who were <u>wrongly implicated</u>
    - He helped them to be <u>free</u>
  5. He ran for <u>parliament</u>
B. His idea for Holmes is <u>vague</u>
    - One of his <u>professors</u>
    - Edgar Allen <u>Poe's character</u>
Conclusion: Holmes was a brilliant man. Doyle was an equally brilliant man.

Page 99

Step 4

    The lecture is about <u>Arthur Conan Doyle's interesting life</u>. He was <u>born in Edinburgh, Scotland</u>. He went to university <u>to be a doctor</u>. He wrote his first story <u>in 1882</u>. It was very popular and was called <u>*A Study in Scarlet*</u>. He became very famous. He used this <u>to help people</u>. He helped people <u>wrongly implicated of crimes</u>. He helped them to be free. Later, he tried to run<u> for parliament</u>. His idea for Holmes is <u>a little bit vague</u>. People say he is based <u>on a professor</u>. Doyle loved to read <u>Edgar Allen Poe's C. August Dupine</u>, so his idea for Holmes may have come from him. Holmes was a brilliant detective. Doyle was also a brilliant man.

Page 100

1. detective   2. partner   3. brilliant
4. clues   5. keen   6. distract
7. preparation   8. unclear

[Unit 9]

Page 101

B

1. The most prominent university in my country is <u>Harvard University</u>.
2. It is located in a <u>big city</u>.
3. I don't want to go to this university because <u>I want to go to a university that is closer to my home</u>.

Page 102

A

1. A good thing about living in a big city is that there are so many things to do.
2. A bad thing about living in a big city is that people can be rude and unfriendly.
3. A good thing about living in a small city is that you can become friends with everyone in the city.
4. A bad thing about living in a small city is that it is easier to speak badly about someone because everyone knows everyone else.

B

Go to nice restaurants
Listen to prominent speakers
Go to concerts
Go to sporting events
Meet people from all around the world
Enjoy the nightlife
Use the good transportation to see surrounding areas

C

Which?   I want to go to <u>Stanford University</u>.
Where?   It is located in <u>Northern California, very close to San Francisco</u>.
What?   I want to study <u>business and history there</u>.
Why?   I want to go to <u>Stanford</u> because <u>it is a great university that gives many opportunities to students who go there</u>.

D

Get good grades
Make excellent friends
Meet people who can help me later
Find a good job
Meet the person I want to marry
Learn new sports
Have a great time
Become more intelligent

Page 103

F

Sample response 1

Reason 1	**Reason 2**
Big cities are busy, and dangerous	Small city has university as focal point of the town
Support	**Support**
Area that surrounds small cities are very safe	So people support the university much more

Conclusion: Want to live in a small city

Sample response 2

Reason 1	**Reason 2**
Big cities are better equipped	Big city universities are usually more prominent
Support	**Support**
Have more things to do like go to museums and concerts	Likely to meet more prominent people

Conclusion: Want to live in a big city

G

1. focal point   2. equipped   3. prominent
4. hesitate   5. Likewise

Page 104

Sample response 1
Step 2

Reason 1	**Reason 2**
Like to be surrounded by people I know well	Big cities have many things that can distract me
Support	**Support**
Big cities have too many people	Have so much to do
	Studies won't be the focal point

Conclusion: Small cities are best for me

Answer Key

Step 3

I want to go to university in <u>a small</u> city. <u>Small cities are best equipped for me because I like to be surrounded by people I know well. Big cities have too many people.</u> Likewise, <u>I hesitate to go to a big city because of all the things that can distract me. Big cities have so much to do, so my studies won't be my focal point.</u> So, <u>small</u> cities are best for me.

Sample response 2
Step 2

Reason 1
Want to get best education possible

Reason 2
Prominent universities create favorable opportunities despite location

Support
The university will ensure students are happy

Support
Important people will come to the university despite the location

Conclusion: Both small and big universities are good for me

Step 3

I want to go to university in <u>any size of city. Both kinds of</u> cities are best equipped for me because <u>I want to get the best education possible. The university will ensure that its students are happy</u>. Likewise, <u>a prominent university will create favorable opportunities despite the location. Important people will come to the university because it is a great university</u>. So, <u>both small and big</u> cities are best for me.

Integrated

Page 105
B
1. A new games room will <u>be built in the dormitory</u>.
2. Students can play <u>pool, cards, and interact with each other in the games room</u>.
3. I think the conversation will be about <u>the benefits of the new games room</u>.

Page 106
B

Man	Woman
• Thinks the games room will <u>be great</u> • Can't wait for <u>it to be finished</u> • Thinks both <u>studying</u> and <u>relaxing</u> are important • Needs <u>a break from academics</u> • Usually goes <u>somewhere else to relax</u> • This is better because <u>he doesn't have to waste time traveling</u> • Can spend free time <u>with other students</u> • Might make <u>new friends</u>	• Doesn't <u>want a new games room</u> • Thinks students should <u>be studying</u> not <u>playing around</u> • Thinks it sounds like <u>fun</u>

Page 107
D

Opinion: The man thinks the new games room is <u>a good idea</u>.
A. It is better because he
   1. won't <u>have to travel to take a break</u>
   2. can take a break and <u>go back to studying</u>
B. The man might
   1. meet <u>new friends</u>
   2. meet <u>other students to study with</u>
C. He thinks the new games room will be <u>beneficial</u>

F
1. interact   2. Hence   3. residents
4. occupied   5. justification

Page 108
Step 2

Woman	Man
• Learns that dorm council is <u>renovating the student lounge</u> and <u>is putting in a new TV and DVD player</u> • Thinks it's <u>a bad idea</u> • Thinks the lounge is for <u>studying and interacting</u> • Knows that people can't <u>interact with the TV on</u> • Usually <u>goes there to study with other students</u> • Thinks it's a <u>good idea</u>	• Thinks it will be <u>beneficial to dorm residents</u> • Believes that more people will <u>go to the lounge to relax</u> • Wants to know <u>what the woman usually does in the lounge</u> • Thinks the woman should <u>write a letter to the dorm advisor and voice her opinion</u>

Page 109

Step 4

Opinion: The woman is <u>not happy about the renovations to the student lounge</u>.
A. The woman thinks the dorm lounge
    1. is for <u>studying</u>.
    2. is not for <u>watching TV</u>
B. She goes there
    1. to <u>study</u>
    2. to <u>work on assignments with other students</u>

Step 5

    The woman is <u>not happy about the proposed changes to the student lounge</u>. She goes there to <u>study</u> not to <u>watch TV</u>. She thinks people can't <u>interact with each other with the TV on</u>. She goes to the lounge to <u>study and work on assignments with other students</u>. She will probably <u>write a letter to the dorm advisor to tell him or her about her opposition</u>.

Check-up

Page 110

1. renovate	2. beneficial	3. advisor
4. opposition	5. favorable	6. surrounds
7. location	8. absolutely	

[Unit 10]

Independent

Page 111

B
1. My favorite art to look at <u>are paintings</u> because <u>they have so many beautiful colors</u>.
2. My favorite art to make <u>are sculptures</u> because <u>I usually get really dirty</u>.
3. The closest art museum to my home is <u>twenty minutes away</u>.

Page 112

A
1. The last art museum that I went to was the Hermitage Museum in St. Petersburg, Russia.
2. I went there two years ago.
3. My favorite things in the museum were the paintings by Michelangelo.
4. I do not want to go back to the museum. It was nice, but I thought that it was boring and not very interesting.

B

Bored	Grand
Interested	Proud
Excited	Sorry
Sad	Happy
Discouraged	Angry

C

What?	I want to improve <u>the parks</u> in my city.
When?	This should happen <u>in the next couple of years</u>.
How?	My city can do this by <u>giving enough money to make sure that the parks are always clean and safe</u>.
Why?	I want to <u>improve the parks</u> because <u>parks are great places to exercise, meet friends, and spend time outside in the sun</u>.

D
Bad schools
Traffic jams
Temporary buildings
Holes in the roads
Bad transportation
Old hospitals
Not enough places for parking
Old, ugly, rundown playgrounds and parks

Page 113

F
Sample response 1

Shouldn't spend money on art and art museums

Reason 1
Waste of money
Support
Doesn't have direct effect on people's lives
Only helps a few people in society

Reason 2
Public money should go to places that have the most societal benefits
Support
Public transportation, schools, roads help everyone

Conclusion: Public money should be used on more important things than art.

Sample response 2

Should spend money on art

Reason 1
Art makes people proud and enriches the lives of people in the city
Support
Grand museum
Helps tourism

Reason 2
Art makes money
Support
Brings in tourists

Conclusion: Art is a great way to make people's lives enjoyable and help the city.

Answer Key

G
1. societal   2. temporary   3. tourism
4. Whereas   5. grand

Page 114

Sample response 1
Step 2

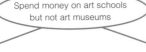

Spend money on art schools but not art museums

Reason 1
Education is a societal need
Support
Education enriches everyone's life
Educated society is a grand society

Reason 2
Museums can be temporary
Support
Can be a huge waste of money

Conclusion: Public money should be used on art schools but not on art museums.

Step 3

   Cities should spend their money on <u>art, but it should be spent on art schools not on art museums</u>. This is because <u>education is a societal need. Education, of all kinds, enriches everyone's life. An educated society is a grand society</u>. In addition, <u>museums can be very temporary. If a museum has to close because no one is visiting it, it is a huge waste of money</u>. Public money should be used on <u>art schools but not on museums</u>.

Sample response 2
Step 2

Spend money on artwork that has a great societal benefit

Reason 1
Is everyone's money
Support
New bridges and buildings help everyone
They make people proud
Museums only help some people

Reason 2
Increases tourism
Support
People will come to see beautiful buildings

Conclusion: Public money should be used on art that can be used by all.

Step 3

   Cities should spend their money on <u>artwork that has a great societal benefit</u>. This is because <u>it is everyone's money. This money should be spent on new grand bridges and buildings that help everyone and makes them proud, whereas museums only help a few people</u>. In addition, <u>beautiful buildings will help to increase tourism as others will come to look at the beautiful architecture</u>. Public money should be used on <u>art that can be appreciated by all</u>.

Page 115

B
1. The US military was first formed in <u>1775</u>.
2. The US armed forces are run by <u>the president of the US</u>.
3. I think that the lecture will be about <u>the history of the US armed forces</u>.

Page 116

B

The US armed forces
- Are seen as <u>the most powerful military in the world</u>
- To join them is <u>voluntary</u>

The US
- Spends more money <u>on it than the rest of the world put together</u>
- Armed forces are made up of <u>the army, marine corps, navy, air force, and coast guard</u>

History of the US military
- Was formed to <u>fight in the War of Independence</u>
- Later took part in <u>the Civil War</u>
- Grew larger in the <u>early twentieth century</u>
- Played a big part in the <u>Allied forces' wins in World War I and II</u>

The US President
- Is the <u>head of all of the armed forces</u>
- The heads of the different parts <u>of the forces help him make decisions</u>

Page 117

D

The lecture and the passage were about <u>the history of the US armed forces</u>.
A. The US armed forces
   1. Formed in <u>1775</u>
   2. Were formed to <u>fight the British in the War of Independence</u>
   3. Later fought in the <u>Civil War</u>
B. The early twentieth century
   1. Forces grew <u>larger</u>
   2. Helped the <u>Allied forces to win World War I and II</u>
C. US armed forces today
   1. Has around <u>1.5 million members</u>
   2. The US spends <u>more money on it than the rest of the world put together</u>
Conclusion: The US armed forces are run by <u>the president of the US</u>.

F
1. voluntary   2. overseas   3. Civil
4. armed forces 5. defense

Page 118
Step 2

The US Coast Guard
- Was formed in 1790
- Its ships protected the US coast

The Modern US Coast Guard
- Set up as a military service and branch of the armed forces
- Main jobs are to protect the public, the environment, and US security interests
- Can do this overseas and in the US
- It is both a life-saving service and an armed force

The Coast Guard in Conflict
- Has been involved in every big US conflict
- Helped to land Allied troops on D-Day in World War II

The Coast Guard Today
- One of its main jobs is port, water-way, and coastal security
- It has around 41, 000 members
- Answers to US Department of Homeland Security

Page 119

Step 4

The passage and lecture were about the US Coast Guard.
A. It was formed in 1790
B. The modern coast guard
  1. Was set up as a military service and branch of the armed forces
  2. Its main missions are to protect the public, the environment, and US security interests
  3. Is both a life-saving service and an armed force
C. Is the smallest of all the armed forces
D. One of its main jobs is port, water-way, and coastal security
E. Is controlled by the US Department of Homeland Security
F. During wars its control is given to the US Navy

Step 5

The passage and lecture were about the US Coast Guard. It was first formed in 1790. Later, the modern Coast Guard was set up as a military service and a branch of the armed forces. Then its main missions were to protect the public, the environment, and US security interests. Today, it is both a life-saving service and an armed force. It is the smallest of all the armed forces and one of its main jobs is port, water-way, and coastal security. It is controlled by the US Department of Homeland Security. In times of war it is controlled by the US Navy.

Check-up

Page 120

1. allied
2. combat
3. independence
4. Coast Guard
5. enriched
6. proud
7. sculptures
8. direct

[Unit 11]

Independent

Page 121

B
1. The name of my group is the National Honor Society.
2. We volunteer and help people who are not as lucky as we are.
3. I continue to be a part of the group because I know that we are helping people to have better lives.

Page 122

A

1. I rarely suggest ideas when I am with a group.
2. I normally don't care when the group does something I don't really want to do.
3. I am usually happier being a regular member of the group.
4. It is important that the group does what I want when I think that the group is going to do something dangerous.

B

Cleaning up   Playing sports
Making something big   Helping other people
Playing games   Going on a trip
Having a party   Going out for dinner

C
When?   I was a leader on my soccer team.
How?   I became the leader by always playing well, and trying my best.
What?   As a leader I always made sure that everyone was trying their hardest.
Why?   I liked being the leader because I enjoyed having the extra responsibility.

D
Instruct other members
Take responsibility
Talk to everyone
Fix controversy
Keep everyone enthusiastic
Give direction
Give incentives to other members
Solve problems

Answer Key

Page 123

F

Sample response 1

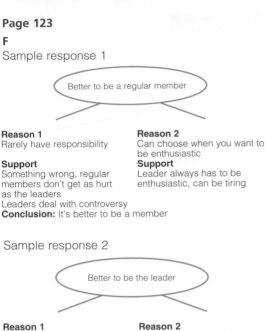

Reason 1
Rarely have responsibility

Support
Something wrong, regular members don't get as hurt as the leaders
Leaders deal with controversy
Conclusion: It's better to be a member

Reason 2
Can choose when you want to be enthusiastic

Support
Leader always has to be enthusiastic, can be tiring

Sample response 2

Better to be the leader

Reason 1
Leaders instruct others on what to do
Support
If there is a problem, leaders can choose to continue or not
Members can't do this

Reason 2
Leaders have more incentive to work hard
Support
They receive more praise if done well
People never dismiss their ideas
Conclusion: Everyone listens to the leader

G
1. incentive   2. enthusiastic   3. instruct
4. dismissed   5. controversy

Page 124

Sample response 1
Step 2

Be A leader, but not THE leader.

Reason 1
It is good
Support
Can instruct other members
Ideas are never dismissed

Reason 2
Don't deal with controversy
Support
Something bad happens, the president must deal with it
Conclusion: Being vice president is the best

Step 3

I think it is better to <u>be a leader, but not THE leader of a group. Maybe something like a vice president</u>. I like this option because <u>it is good to instruct other members, and I know that my ideas will never be dismissed</u>. But the best part is <u>that the vice president doesn't have to deal with controversy all the time. When something bad happens, the president must deal with it. Being vice president</u> is the best.

Sample response 2
Step 2

Working alone

Reason 1
Groups have problems
Support
Always controversy
People don't like to work with other members

Reason 2
Working alone is better
Support
Do what I want
Ideas never dismissed
No one instructs me on what to do
Lots of incentive to work and be enthusiastic

Conclusion: Working alone is the best

Step 3

I think it is better to <u>work alone than in a group at all</u>. I like this option because <u>groups have many problems. There always seems to be controversy, and people don't always like to work with other members</u>. But the best part <u>of working alone is that I can do what I want. My ideas are never dismissed. No one ever instructs me on what to do, and I have a lot of incentive to be enthusiastic because it is my project. Working alone</u> is the best.

Integrated

Page 125

B
1. The students are discussing <u>all the work the man has to do</u>.
2. The man has <u>a lot of school work and he has to work at his job</u>.
3. I think the rest of the conversation will be about <u>how he can reduce the amount of work that he has to do</u>.
4. I think the man should <u>quit /keep his job while he's in school</u>.

Page 126

A

Man	Woman
• Has <u>a lot of work but not enough time</u> • Both school <u>and his job are really busy</u> • Student needs <u>his job to make money for rent</u> • Doesn't want <u>to have a lot of debt after university</u> • Will probably <u>skip some classes to finish his work</u>	• Thinks he <u>should quit his job</u> • Recommends that he <u>get a loan for money</u> • Thinks of a loan as <u>an investment in his future</u> • Future job will <u>be good and he can earn a lot of money</u> • Should check <u>if there is an attendance requirement for his classes</u>

B
1. The man <u>wants to keep his job because it's important to have money to pay his rent and tuition</u>.

2. The woman thinks <u>he can get a loan to pay his</u> <u>rent and he will make money in the future if he</u> <u>gets a good job. Also, there might be an</u> <u>attendance requirement in his classes</u>.

Page 127
D
The conversation is about <u>the man's busy schedule</u>.
A. Woman's reasons why he should quit his job
   1. School is <u>important</u>
   2. University is <u>an investment in his future</u>
   3. A good education will <u>help him get a job</u> <u>and earn money in the future</u>
B. Man's reasons to keep his job
   1. Thinks he should <u>skip classes to finish his</u> <u>work</u>
   2. Believes he can <u>work and go to school</u>
   3. Doesn't want <u>to have a lot of debt when he</u> <u>finishes school</u>
Conclusion: I think <u>he should quit his job</u> because <u>it's not as important as his education</u>.

E
Conclusion: I think <u>he should keep his job</u> because <u>it's important to learn how to balance different parts</u> <u>of your life and he needs the money</u>.

G
1. accumulation
2. journal
3. shift
4. investments
5. Sociology

Page 128
Step 1

Advantages	Disadvantages
• It's a good way to <u>save</u> <u>money</u> • Can earn <u>more money over</u> <u>time</u> • Will become <u>more</u> <u>responsible with money</u>	• Can't <u>get money at any time</u> • Banks may charge <u>a fee to</u> <u>take out the money early</u> • Could <u>lose money</u> if <u>you</u> <u>choose a bad investment</u>

Step 3
The conversation is about <u>investing money</u>.
A. The advantages of investing are that
   1. you can <u>save a lot of money</u>
   2. it's possible to earn <u>more money</u>
   3. you may become <u>more responsible with</u> <u>money</u>
B. The disadvantages of investing are that
   1. you can't <u>take out money at any time</u>
   2. banks may <u>charge a fee to take out money</u> <u>early</u>

3. it's possible to <u>lose money if you choose a</u> <u>bad investment</u>
Conclusion: I think <u>the student should keep her</u> <u>money in the bank because it's safer and easier</u> <u>to access</u>.

Page 129
Step 4
   The conversation is about <u>students investing</u> <u>money</u>. Investing can be good because <u>you can</u> <u>save your money easily</u>. In fact, you can <u>also earn</u> <u>more money quickly</u> and <u>become more</u> <u>responsible with your money</u>. Some disadvantages are <u>that you can't get your money quickly if you</u> <u>need it. The bank may charge you a fee to take it</u> <u>out early. Also, if you choose a dangerous</u> <u>investment, you could lose your money</u>.

   I think <u>the student should keep her money in</u> <u>the bank because it's safer and easier to access.</u> <u>Then she</u> <u>doesn't have to worry about it</u>.

   I think <u>the student should invest her money</u> <u>because it's worth the risk to earn lots of money. If</u> <u>she has lots of money her life will be easier</u>.

Check-up
Page 130
1. skip	2. requirement	3. double
4. boss	5. rarely	6. extremely
7. continue	8. member	

[Unit 12]

Independent
Page 131
B
1. I <u>bought a new computer</u>.
2. It made me feel <u>bad because I didn't need to</u> <u>get a new computer</u>.
3. I did this because <u>my friend was talking about</u> <u>how great his new computer was</u>.

Page 132
A
1. I saw an advertisement for a new kind of orange juice.
2. In the advertisement a famous singer sang and danced to a bottle of orange juice.
3. I laughed at the advertisement.
4. I did not follow the advice of the advertisement because I do not like the singer and do not want to buy the orange juice.

B

Parents	Best friend
Pastor	Teacher
Favorite athlete	Grandparent
Favorite movie star	Favorite singer

C

Who?   I talk to <u>my brothers</u>.

How long?   I start making my decision <u>two weeks before I must decide</u>.

What?   I get the best information from <u>television</u>.

Why?   I trust this information because <u>on TV they always have a very smart person who gives advice to a lot of people</u>.

D

How long it takes

How much it costs

How will it help me?

Will I really enjoy it?

Would I rather do something else?

Can I do something else that is similar?

Page 133

F

Sample response 1

Reason 1
Watch a lot of TV
Support
Always someone telling me to do something
Difficult to resist

Reason 2
Overwhelms me
Support
Eventually give in because I hear it so much

Conclusion: That is why I think TV is most influential

Sample response 2

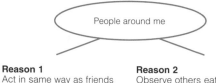

Reason 1
Act in same way as friends and family
Support
Speak and use similar vocabulary
Want to fit in

Reason 2
Observe others eating and dressing in certain way
Support
They want to fit in as well

Conclusion: I certainly am influenced by people around me

G

1. observe   2. vocabulary   3. overwhelm

4. actions   5. attribute

Page 134

Sample response 1

Step 2

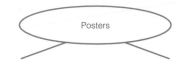

Reason 1
Observe them everywhere

Support
Makes me think about them
Often give in because I thought about it so much
Conclusion: Posters are very influential

Reason 2
Have famous and beautiful people on them
Support
Want to have same actions as famous people so do what they are doing in the poster

Step 3

    I think that <u>giant posters</u> are the most influential. This is because <u>I observe these everywhere. This makes me think about and look at the posters. Often I give in because I have seen and thought about it so much</u>. It is also influential because <u>they often have famous and beautiful people on it. I try to have my actions be similar to those of famous people, so I often do what they are doing on the poster. Posters</u> are very influential.

Sample response 2

Step 2

Things in the mail

Reason 1
Often get overwhelmed

Support
Can be frustrating, but effective
Conclusion: Things in the mail are very influential

Reason 2
Use vocabulary that is attributed to success
Support
Want to be successful

Step 3

    I think that <u>letters, advertisements, etc. in the mail</u> are the most influential. This is because <u>I often get overwhelmed with things in my mailbox. It can certainly be frustrating, but I think it is effective.</u> It is also influential because <u>they use vocabulary in the letters that are often attributed to being successful. I certainly want to be successful so I do as they want. Things in the mail</u> are very influential.

Integrated

Page 135

B

1. Scientists thought that only humans <u>could use verbal communication</u>.

2. Scientists who disagreed began to <u>study the vervet monkey</u>.

3. I think the scientists found out that <u>there are many different animals that use verbal communication</u>.

Page 136

A

- The vervet monkey also uses verbal communication.
- They live <u>in Africa in small groups within a small amount of territory</u>.
- They have many <u>enemies</u>.
- The vervet has a loud <u>oral shriek</u>.
- Scientists analyzed <u>the shrieks</u>.
- They are used to <u>caution other vervets</u>.
- Each shriek <u>has an apparent meaning</u>.
- One shriek means <u>there is an eagle</u>.
- Another shriek means <u>there is a jaguar</u>.
- It is important <u>to run to the right place</u>.
- Vervets have a vocabulary <u>of about ten words</u>.
- It seems humans and vervets both use verbal communication.

B

1. They learned that <u>vervets also use verbal communication. They use oral shrieks to communicate with each other</u>.
2. They need to communicate because <u>many other animals in the jungle want to eat them. It is very dangerous for vervets</u>.

Page 137

D

The lecture is about <u>the vervet monkey</u>.
A. The vervet
  1. has <u>many enemies</u>
  2. lives <u>in small groups in the jungle</u>
B. Vervets make <u>loud, oral shrieks</u>
C. The shrieks are used to <u>caution other vervets</u>
  1. One shriek means <u>eagle</u>
  2. Another shriek means <u>jaguar</u>
D. The vervet must run to <u>the right place to be safe</u>
E. The vervet has a vocabulary of <u>about ten words</u>
Conclusion: Humans and vervets both seem to use verbal communication.

F

1. oral   2. evaluations   3. territory
4. caution   5. apparent

Page 138
Step 1

- Vervets' verbal communication is difficult to understand.

- Many people do not hear <u>any apparent difference in the shrieks</u>.
- Some scientists thought vervets <u>did not talk to each other</u>.
- Scientists used computers to <u>analyze the shrieks</u>.
- The shrieks were <u>different</u>.
- They first learned that shrieks were <u>a caution to their friends</u>.
- Scientists put <u>speakers in the jungles in bushes and trees</u>.
- They played the tapes and watched <u>what the vervets did.</u>
- Scientists want to study <u>other monkeys to see if they can talk</u>.
- Other monkeys live <u>in large territories</u>.
- Vervets are small, smart, and <u>live close together, so they are easy to study</u>.
- Scientists have learned a lot from <u>vervets</u>.

Step 3

The lecture is about vervets' verbal communication.
A. Difficult to understand
  1. Many people could not hear <u>any difference in their shrieks</u>.
  2. Scientists did not think vervets could <u>speak to each other</u>.
B. Used Computers
  1. Computers <u>analyzed the shrieks</u>.
  2. Final evaluation showed <u>that the shrieks were different</u>.
C. Scientists studied the meanings by
  1. Putting <u>speakers in the jungle</u>
  2. Watching <u>to see what the vervets did</u>
D. Studying
  1. Other monkeys are difficult to study because <u>they live in large areas</u>.
  2. Vervets are easy <u>to study</u>.
Scientists have learned <u>a lot from vervets</u>.

Page 139
Step 4

The lecture is about <u>vervets' verbal communication</u>. Vervets are difficult to understand. Many people <u>could not hear any difference in their shrieks</u>. Some scientists <u>didn't think that they could talk</u>. The scientists used computers to <u>analyze the shrieks. They learned the shrieks were different</u>. Scientists learned the meanings of the shrieks by <u>putting speakers in the jungle and watching the vervets</u>. They want to study other monkeys, but <u>it is very difficult to study them because they live in larger areas. However, vervets are easy to study</u>. They have taught <u>scientists a lot</u>.

Answer Key

Check-up

Page 140

1. jungle
2. bushes
3. shriek
4. meaning
5. certainly
6. gave in
7. fit in
8. etc.

[Review 2]

Independent 1

Page 141

Sample response 1
Step 2

First reason
Get an education

Second Reason
Better job opportunities when finished

Like to
Make new friends
Conclusion: Attending university is better

Step 3

I think it is best to <u>attend university</u> when I graduate high school. I would like to <u>attend university</u> because <u>it will give me a chance to make new friends</u>. I think this is the best idea because I will <u>get an education and I will have better job opportunities when I graduate</u>.

Sample response 2
Step 2

First reason
Make money
Like to
Work and not sit in class
Conclusion: Getting a job is better

Second Reason
Don't have to go to school

Step 3

I think it is best to <u>get a job</u> when I graduate high school. I would like to <u>get job</u> because <u>it will allow me to work and I don't have to sit in a classroom</u>. I think this is the best idea because I will <u>make money and I don't have to go to school</u>.

Integrated 1

Page 142
Step 2

Sign Language
- Used by <u>adults and children who are deaf or hard of hearing</u>
- A language that uses <u>hand motions and body language</u>
- Dates back to <u>the eighteenth century</u>
- Varies <u>between countries</u>
- Classes are offered at <u>university</u>
- People who study sign language are usually <u>looking for a career using sign language</u>
- A good career is <u>a translator</u>
- The most common sign is "<u>I love you</u>"
- Libraries and bookstores have <u>great books for beginners</u>

Page 143
Step 4

The passage and lecture are about <u>sign language</u>.
A. Sign language
   1. started in <u>the eighteenth century in Europe</u>
   2. is used by <u>people who are deaf or that are hard of hearing</u>
B. Universities offer classes if <u>there are enough students who want to participate</u>
C. A career using sign language is <u>to become a translator</u>
D. The most common sign is "<u>I love you</u>"
E. Bookstores and libraries have <u>books for beginners who want to learn sign language</u>

Step 5

The passage and lecture are about <u>sign language</u>. Sign language started in the <u>eighteenth century in Europe</u>. It is used by people <u>who are deaf or hard of hearing</u>. Often universities offer classes if <u>there are enough students who want to participate. Becoming a translator</u> is a career option for someone who wants to pursue sign language. The most common universal sign in sign language is for "<u>I love you</u>." Bookstores and libraries are great places to find <u>books for beginners who want to learn the language</u>.

Integrated 2

Page 144

Step 1

Man	Woman
• Asks woman <u>what she is working on</u>	• The woman is working on <u>college applications</u>
• <u>Overwhelmed</u> by college applications	• Asks <u>what he might do</u>
• Thinking about <u>traveling</u> or joining <u>armed forces</u>	• Thought he was interested in <u>architecture</u>
• Doesn't want to <u>regret not</u> traveling	• <u>Studying abroad</u> will give chance to travel
• Still plans to <u>fill out applications</u>	• Wishes him good luck

Step 3

The conversation is about <u>a student having to make a decision between attending university and not attending university</u>.
A. The student must choose whether <u>he wants to go to university or if he wants to do something else like join the armed forces</u>
B. Not attending university
   1. Can join <u>armed forces</u>
   2. Or <u>travel</u>
C. If he goes to university
   1. He can <u>always study abroad</u>
   2. He is too <u>overwhelmed</u> to make a decision

Conclusion: I would prefer <u>to go to university and study abroad because I would still get a chance to travel and I would be able to get an education. I could always do more traveling during the summer while I'm not in school or when I graduate from university</u>.

Conclusion: I would prefer <u>to not go to university when I graduate because I want to do something where I can travel. I want to join the armed forces or just travel while I am still young. I can always go to university later</u>.

Page 145

Step 4

   The conversation is about <u>a student having to make a decision between attending university or not attending university</u>. The student must choose whether <u>he wants to go to university or if he wants to do something else like join the armed</u> forces. If he does not attend university, he can join the <u>armed forces</u> or <u>travel</u>. If he goes to university, he can <u>study abroad</u> and still go to school.

Independent 2

Page 146

Step 2

Sample response 1

First reason	**Second Reason**
Easier to dance to	Has good beats
Better because	
The sound of hip hop makes it easier to dance	
Conclusion: Hip hop is the best for dancing.	

Step 3

   I think people should listen to <u>hip hop if they want to dance</u>. It is usually a lot more enjoyable to <u>dance to music that has good beats</u>. This allows people to <u>dance and not feel so awkward</u>. <u>Hip hop</u> music is <u>the best for dancing</u>.

Sample response 2

Classical or opera

First reason	**Second Reason**
Relaxing	Talented musicians
Better because	
It is relaxing and fun to listen to such talented musicians	
Conclusion: Classical music or opera is easy to relax to and enjoyable.	

Step 3

   I think people should listen to <u>classical or opera music</u>. It is usually a lot more enjoyable to <u>relax to</u>. This allows people to <u>enjoy talented musicians and relax to enjoyable music</u>. <u>Classical</u> music is the <u>easiest to relax to</u>.